Published by the Association for a Swiss Migration Museum. Edited by Bruno Abegg and Barbara Lüthi

Small Number Big Impact

Swiss Immigration to the USA

Neue Zürcher Zeitung Publishing

Contributors

Bruno Abegg, Bernard R. Bachmann, Mathias Braschler, Thomas Buomberger,
Tiberio Cardu, Bänz Friedli, Grafilu, Erika Hebeisen, Anne Hoffmann,
Annelise Leuenberger, Marius Leutenegger, Barbara Lüthi, Stephan Lütolf,
Guido Magnaguagno, Roland Müller, Rafaël Newman, Walter Niederberger,
Barbara Rettenmund, Heiner Ritzmann, Jacques Sandoz, Leo Schelbert,
Jürg Schneider, Urs Widmer.

Partners of the exhibition:
Presence Switzerland and the Swiss National Museum

The Association for a Swiss Migration Museum would like to express its gratitude to its project partners for their commitment, their assistance, and their generous support for the exhibition on Ellis Island and in the Swiss National Museum. Particular thanks are due to Presence Switzerland for its financial support of the English edition of this book.

The editors and publisher thank the following for their generous support of the English edition of this book:

City of Winterthur
Foundation for Migration, Population and Environment
Foundation of the Families Vontobel
Migros-Kulturprozent
Organisation of the Swiss Abroad
Sandoz Family Foundation
Swiss Society of New York
Winterthur Cultural Foundation
Zurich Anniversary Foundation

Bibliographic information published by Die Deutsche Bibliothek
Die Deutsche Bibliothek lists this publication in the Deutsche Nationalbibliografie; detailed bibliographic data are available on the Internet at http://dnb.de.

Title of the German edition:
"Small Number – Big Impact"
Schweizer Einwanderung in die USA
Copyright © 2006 by Verlag Neue Zürcher Zeitung, Zurich

Translated by
Rafaël Newman

ISBN 10: 3-03823-260-2
ISBN 13: 978-3-03823-260-5

www.nzz-libro.ch
NZZ Libro is an imprint of the Neue Zürcher Zeitung.

www.migrationsmuseum.ch
(information about the exhibition "Small Number – Big Impact," museum project and membership)

Preface

The brilliant physicist Albert Einstein was born a German, became a Swiss, and died an American. In its issue dated December 31, 1999, Time magazine featured him as "Person of the Century" – ahead of Franklin D. Roosevelt and Mahatma Gandhi. But while all three of the countries mentioned above would gladly claim Einstein's achievements as those of one of its citizens, Einstein was not German, Swiss or American – he was a migrant.

Migrants carry their history and culture with them on their travels. And, as the diverse accounts of immigration contained in this book make plain, they enrich their new homes. It is one of the features of the U.S. that new arrivals immediately become Americans. For this reason, we Swiss would like to lay a little more stress on the fact that figures like Jewel Kilcher and Bob Lutz have Swiss roots. But it might also be of interest to Americans to learn this, as they continue to go by the clichés (as true as they may be) of Switzerland as the bestower of cheese, yodeling, watches and chocolate. The fact is, however, that Switzerland has also given the U.S. automotive entrepreneurs like Chevrolet, bridge-builders like Ammann, computer specialists like Hölzle, hockey goalies like Aebischer, football stars like Roethlisberger and Hollywood directors like Forster. One Swiss emigrant even teaches Americans about their very own home-grown culture, the blues.

So while the actual number of Swiss immigrants to the U.S. may be small, their impact is big.

At the Association for a Swiss Migration Museum, we are interested in the way immigrants shape their new countries – and this from the perspective of Switzerland as the recipient of such benefits. Our main goal is to create a vibrant new museum, a center for exhibitions about the country of immigrants and emigrants that is Switzerland and the forge for a new Swiss identity, comparable with Ellis Island.

For just as many Swiss (and their descendants) have contributed to U.S. vitality, so too has Switzerland profited from the special skills of countless immigrants. It really doesn't matter which nationality is listed in their passports. For us, therefore, Switzerland in the 21st century is part of an open global community, one that has recognized the importance of migration for prosperous development.

We would like to thank all those whose contributions to our book have helped to make these crucial episodes in the history of Swiss emigration to the U.S. available to a broad readership.

We also thank our partners in this project, Presence Switzerland and the Swiss National Museum, as well as our generous sponsors.

It pays to take a closer look at the United Switzerlands of America.

In the name of the Association for a Swiss Migration Museum

Samir   Markus Hodel

President   Managing Director

Foreword

"Let us be united, as two sister republics," wrote Jean-Rodolphe Valltravers, a scholar from Biel, in April of 1778 to Benjamin Franklin, with whom he corresponded. Since that date, the United States of America has been joined with Switzerland by a bond of sisterhood that goes beyond the similarities of the two countries' constitutions, drafted respectively in 1787 and 1848. A further parallel between Switzerland and the U.S. is the fact that both nations have a vibrant history of immigration.

Situated at the heart of Europe, Switzerland has grown over time from a loose assembly of peoples into a multicultural federalist community. Celt, Roman, Austrian, French, the traces of Switzerland's various visitors are all still visible, both culturally and demographically. Today, 21 percent of the Swiss population is foreign. And, counting "mixed" marriages and the second and third generations of immigrants, almost half of Switzerland has a personal encounter with migration in its family tree, a proportion that is well exceeded in America.

Thousands of our own citizens have been among those making the trans-Atlantic voyage, seeking their fortune in America in great numbers since the early 18th century. Some were driven by curiosity and the hope of a better future, while others were simply forced into exile by the contemporary vagaries of the Swiss economy. We can be proud of figures like Albert Gallatin, Johann August Sutter and Louis Chevrolet, who did so much for the New World. More recently, of course, Ben Roethlisberger has shown what Swiss roots can do, leading his team, the Pittsburgh Steelers, to victory at the Super Bowl, the youngest quarterback in history to do so!

At the same time, we are grateful to our own immigrants for their enormous contribution to the creation of a modern Switzerland. It was an Englishman and a German, for instance, who founded Brown Boveri, today's ABB, while the Ciba chemical company was started by a Frenchman, and a German laid the foundations of Nestlé, now a global player. And the list goes on and on. But if one thing above all has left its mark on Swiss culture, it is the legendary "American Way of Life," more present than ever now in the form of Google and Starbucks, as well-known in their way as Elvis, Mickey Mouse, George Clooney, hamburgers and hotdogs.

Together with its partners, Presence Switzerland and the Swiss National Museum, the Association for a Swiss Migration Museum has organized an exhibition on Swiss immigration to the United States.

"Small Number – Big Impact," to open on this year's Swiss national holiday, will be on show for three months at New York's Ellis Island Immigration Museum. It is no accident that the exhibition was prepared under the aegis of the "swiss roots" campaign; after all, the aim of that project is to connect Americans of Swiss descent with the country of their ancestors, and thus to encourage dialog between two foreign cultures with so much in common. As a "swiss roots" partner, the Association for a Swiss Migration Museum hopes that this book will raise awareness of the extent to which countries can profit from their immigrants.

I support the aims of the "swiss roots" campaign, and I welcome the exhibition at Ellis Island's celebrated Immigration Museum. And I would be delighted if as many Americans as possible, both with and, of course, without Swiss roots, would take this opportunity to get to know a piece of their own immigration history.

Micheline Calmy-Rey
Federal Councillor and Head of the Swiss Federal Department of Foreign Affairs

Barbara Lüthi

Stories That Made History

Promised Land? Sodom and Gomorrah? A country of dreams or of nightmares? There have always been a thousand different reasons to leave Switzerland for the United States – poverty, religion, ideology, the will to freedom, a sense of mission, a taste for adventure, persecution, career planning, the call of science, the thirst for knowledge, the pioneering spirit, a love of sports, love all on its own, of course, and plain old compulsion: there was a time, after all, when Switzerland simply shipped its outlaws off to America. There have always been a thousand reasons for emigrants' success, and a thousand others for their failure. There is no one single phenomenon that could be referred to as "Swiss emigration to the U.S." – there have been a thousand different emigrations. This book illuminates individual destinies, with portraits of figures both historic and current, both celebrated and (until now) virtually unknown, both heavyweights and lightweights; read continuously, they provide a glimpse of the big picture, of the effect Swiss immigrants and their descendants have had on the United States. And the impact they had was not trivial.

When do people realize they must leave the place they have come to call home? How do they find their way in a strange land? Where does the appetite, the drive to emigrate come from? These are tricky questions, and there are no definitive answers to them. All we know for certain is that migration is as much a part of the human condition as birth, sickness and death, and that people have been traversing stretches of land, crossing oceans and borders, and moving around within their national and regional boundaries since the beginning of time. The trade routes of the Middle Ages and the early modern period in Europe, the age of colonialism, the movements of nomadic tribes and the mass migrations of the industrial era: for centuries human beings have been striking camp and settling elsewhere before, as often as not, moving on or returning to their place of origin. The notion of a process, of the potential for transformation is present in the Latin stem of our word "migration," *migro,* meaning to remove, depart or change.

Two elements in particular distinguish the mass migrations of the 19th and 20th centuries from those of earlier periods. For one thing, there was the sheer volume of people set in motion by an increasingly global capitalism; for another, the new efficiency of transportation, by steamer, railway and airplane, as well as the improved roads and lower cost of travel had simplified movement. Migration, whether motivated by the search for employment or the flight from oppression, developed into a phenomenon of hitherto unknown proportions.

Swiss migration was triggered by factors typical of other European countries as well, including the successive waves of poverty throughout practically the entire course of the 19th century, the rise of factories and the shifts of population to industrial centers. Switzerland in this period was a-bustle with men and women of various nationalities, religions, social classes and age groups.

On the road since the beginning

Swiss people migrated to many different places. The most celebrated of this company are the mercenaries of the late medieval period, known as *Reisläufer;* the pastry chefs who started to leave Graubünden for European capitals in the 17th century; the Ticinese gold-diggers setting off for Australia and California beginning in the 1850s; and the simultaneous mass exodus from parts of German-speaking Switzerland to Brazilian coffee plantations.

Salman Rushdie has described the immigrant as "the central or defining figure of the twentieth century." A glance at Swiss immigration to the U.S. casts this observation in a new light. While phases of emigration may have been a feature of the early modern period, the major migrations from Switzerland to the U.S. took place in the 19th century, with peaks in the years 1851–55 and 1880-84. As for the 20th century, it was only in the aftermath of the First World War that Switzerland saw its citizens leaving home in truly large numbers. From 1789 to 1914, some half a million Swiss went abroad, and around 200,000 emigrated between 1920 and 2000. They were headed mainly for the U.S., followed by Argentina and Brazil, at least in the 19th and early 20th centuries. Those who left in the 19th century were on the whole fleeing agricultural crisis and famine. By the 1920s the popularity among Swiss of the U.S. as "the land of unlimited opportunity" was already on the wane, what with the economic upturn at home, the American quota system, which restricted entrance permits for various nationalities and "races," as well as the consequences of the First World War and, eventually, the Second. The rise of the airlines encouraged reverse immigration, both temporary and permanent, especially after the Second World War, trans-Atlantic traffic in the direction of the U.S. declined, and migration was increasingly dictated by professional exigencies.

Migration is never a predictable process: it ultimately resists complete control. The unknown, the coincidental and the unexpected are all risks associated with planning one's departure, one's travel and arrival. In earlier days, without the media's brokerage of the world we have now come to expect, it was for the most part a voyage into terra incognita, replete with surprises both positive and negative. A Swiss emigrant makes the following report in a letter dated 1711: "As to my situation, I am well and live happily and would not wish to have stayed at home. As to the country, is such that he that has riches, gold and silver, can be a gentleman just like in Europe. But I tell you, for a poor man or a working man it is better like here. If he wants to do day labor, he will get half a crown every day in produce or livestock; gold and silver are scarce. Land he can get as much as he needs. Cattle and pigs he can get as many as he can handle...The land is hot, uncultivated, many streams of water, great forests. The natives or Indians are black, half naked, but good natured. Yet to be hoped the land will be rather fruitful, but I do not advise nor cause anyone to move here because of the costly and wearisome voyage across the cruel and wild sea; but I for my part did not find it hard although for old people and young children it is wearisome." [Jackob Währen von Zweysimmen, *Aus America oder India,* d. 9. Aprillis 1711 = From America or India, April 9, 1711] A difficult journey, new horizons, undreamt-of riches. But migration can also mean the loss of the familiar, encounters with strangers, and insurmountable obstacles, as Samuel Dyssli makes clear in a 1737 letter from Carolina to family and friends back home: "To report about the nature of the country, I want to warn everybody not to hanker after coming to this country, for sicknesses do far too much harm here and people die in droves, often the parents and children, then the children are sent away, one here, the other there, and are kept like slaves and raised in ignorance like Savages. They also no longer give provisions to the newcomers as they used to. And also everything is cruelly dear...Carolina looks more like a land of blackamoors than a land occupied by whites...Meantime I say once again, let no one be tempted into this land. Surely there are people that I know have come to Switzerland and had roguish letters on them as if it were so good in Carolina, but it is a damned deceit. If one man is doing well, 1000 others are that much worse off. As I said before, I am now so well off, thank God, it would be a sin to ask for more. But what of it, one swallow does not make a spring." [Carlestatt in Carolina, den 3to Christmonat 1737 = December 3, 1737] A century later, an immigrant wrote from St. Louis that "the climate here differs greatly from that in Switzerland," and made one sick. He went on to note that people had to look out for themselves in the New World, and that there were many causes for complaint: "Life in America has nuts that not every-one can crack." And again, some months later: "Oh that I could shout it in everybody's ear and heart: Do stay at home, you who are able to get along in Switzerland." [Anonymous, St. Louis, April 29 and July 20, 1849] Letters from emigrants to those who have remained behind continue to be filled with reports of illnesses and the climate, the struggle for one's daily bread, and longing for home, and this well into the 20th century; but they also contain accounts of successes, fascinating novelties and interest aroused. Some are fearful of emigration, while others sense the opportunity for change. The motives for departure turn up in the most unlikely company, poverty paired with ideology, the desire for adventure coupled with discrimination, caree-rism combined with simple curiosity.

Sister Republics

But it wasn't only the Swiss who dreamed about the U.S.; the mythologizing went the other way as well, and still does. Many Americans cherished an idealized image of Switzerland during the 19th century. The myth of Switzerland as an "alpine sister republic" was born. The two federal democratic states were half critical, half romantic in each other's regard during this period, which doubtless said a great deal about the self-image of each.

As early as the end of the 17th and particularly during the 18th century, prior to independence and amid the debate about a new form for the confederation, British Americans were having a good look at the few re-publics already in operation. Because Switzerland enjoyed considerable political allure in the 18th century, Federalists and Anti-Federalists alike made reference to the teachings and writings of Swiss thinkers as they discussed the American constitution, as well as to the federalist structure of Switzerland as it existed at the time.

Switzerland served the U.S. as a political model in the founding period of the American republic. In his *Common Sense,* published in 1776, Thomas Paine (1737–1809) made the case for severing the American colonies from England with somewhat anachronistic reference to the republican forms of both Switzerland and the Netherlands, and the domestic and foreign peace enjoyed by both countries as a result. That same year, John Witherspoon (1723–1794) argued in similar terms in a debate at the Continental Congress, to which he was a delegate: its federal character had helped Switzerland to avoid internal confessional conflicts and wars, he maintained, and should provide America with a political blueprint.

It is quite probable that not a few Swiss fought against the British in the war of independence, although since they were often classed with the Germans, the precise number will never be known. While Jean Jacques Rousseau's influence on the American Revolution was relatively slight, the ideas of two other Swiss intellec-tuals, Jean Jacques Burlamaqui (1694–1748), of Geneva, and Emer de Vattel (1714–1767), of Neuchâtel, en-joyed a warm reception. Switzerland (along with the Netherlands) was again the model consulted when

the Americans needed a republican-federalist system of organization. Founding fathers Thomas Jefferson (1743–1826), Alexander Hamilton (1755–1804) and James Madison (1751–1836) studied Swiss government, each from a different point of view. More than anyone else, however, the future President of the United States John Adams (1735–1826) argued for Swiss-style political organization – without ever having visited Switzerland himself. Adams had recourse to various travelers' accounts of Swiss cantonal constitutions as he elaborated his position during the Philadelphia Convention of 1787, at which the new American constitution was debated and Switzerland served as a pivotal reference generally.

At the dawn of the 19th century, the Switzerland already established in American minds was a fully idealized image of a patriotic and peaceful land subsisting in "the spirit of liberty." The icon was nourished constantly by the reports of travelers. "Of all places I have seen in my travels this pleases me the most. The wealthy and contented appearance of these happy people declares this to be the land of liberty. Everything here is gay cheerful and happy and everything proclaims the superiority of the republican over every other sort of government. May such a one ever prevail in our Country is my sincere wish," wrote a politician and delegate to the 1787 Constitutional Convention in a letter to Thomas Jefferson dated August 30, 1788. In the ensuing century, American visitors to Switzerland were particularly fascinated by its landscapes and mountain life. The mythologized picture of raw nature and the pristine, "authentic" lifestyle of the patriotic alpine folk was formed during this period, and often amplified in works of literature. World-famous for her *Uncle Tom's Cabin* (1852), the writer and abolitionist Harriet Beecher Stowe (1811–1896) grew rapturous in her memories of Switzerland: "Ah, they breathe a pure air, these generous Swiss, among these mountain tops! May their simple words be a prophecy divine." But it was more than simply Switzerland that was being beatified. The figure of William Tell was already revered by Americans prior to the declaration of independence in 1776, and his story was industriously mounted as a drama and retold as literature before the century was out. He was represented as the "son of liberty" and the "Noble Mountaineer," the embodiment of the triumph of national independence fitted out with respectable virtues – indeed, for want of a native tradition in the infancy of the republic, Tell may have served many Americans as a figurehead.

When Napoleon invaded Switzerland, many of its trans-Atlantic admirers thought they were witnessing "the violent destruction of a golden age" (Urs Hammer). The Ancien Régime had been idealized in parallel with the simple, modest, patriotic, hard-working mountain folk. As late as the end of the 19th century, the otherwise dependably ironic Mark Twain (1835–1910) had the following words of blissful admiration for Switzerland as he recalled his journey through various European countries: "This is a good atmosphere to be in, morally as well as physically. After trying the political atmosphere of the neighboring monarchies, it is healing and refreshing to breathe in the air that has known no taint of slavery for six hundred years ... "

Of course, criticism of Switzerland was also voiced as early as the mid-19th century, including evocations of the dangers of decadence, collective moral degradation and the ruin of the balance between humanity and nature driven by a nascent mass tourism. Despite continuing admiration for its system of direct democracy and the idea of a "freedom-loving mountain people," the American eye was increasingly trained on other aspects of Switzerland, that prosperous, model modern state whose famous banks had circled the wagons to defend their ill-gotten gains. Switzerland's image in the U.S. was damaged during the 1990s in the discussion of Swiss banks' Holocaust culpability. And yet Switzerland seems to have remained the very picture of

precision and purity in the American imaginary, to judge by an advertising campaign of The Coffee Bean & Tea Leaf restaurant chain promising "100% chemical free SWISS WATER."

Small Number – Big Impact

Compared to that of the Irish, Italians or Poles, Swiss immigration to the U.S. has not been enormous. But it has featured some outstanding figures, such as the bridge-builder Othmar Ammann, the film-maker Marc Forster, the physician Elisabeth Kübler-Ross and the politician Albert Gallatin, while Adolph Rickenbacher could boast that he had created the number one icon of U.S. pop culture, the electric guitar. Like their fellow immigrants from all other countries and ethnicities, Swiss people helped build the United States. And while this may be of greater interest to the Swiss than to the Americans, 99% of whom are themselves immigrants or descendants of immigrants, the vibrant diversity of biographies that makes of the U.S. a "nation of immigrants," one of the pillars of its international identity, is also a Swiss accomplishment.

This book is first and foremost a collection of such biographies, assembled in their tangible materiality to provide some insight into the motives and desires of emigrants. Countless interviews, letters, official decrees and dossiers, in dusty archives, private estates and other *lieux de mémoire,* all document individual life histories. And while most migrants have left barely a trace, the retelling of selected biographies from various centuries makes plain the value of studying *individual* destinies even in the age of *mass* migration. These discrete stories, after all, bear the sediments of subjective perceptions and collective horizons of expectation as well as of human social relations. Biographical accounts narrate both the self and the world, hope and disappointment, success and failure, all united in the form of individual destiny. The foreseeable meets the accidental, strategies encounter blows of fate. For those of us who can only read such accounts as epigones, these stories sometimes seem to come from beyond our temporal and spatial realm.

Pictures and photographs also tell of the past. At first glance, people in photographs look so near at hand, almost as if we could touch them – and yet they are so far away. With their promise of authenticity, photographs possess the ability to immediately consign their subjects to the past; they perform a kind of temporal fixation, even if they seem primarily to function as epistemological instruments. One of the duties of photography, according to Susan Sontag, is to reveal the world in all its variety, and to train our senses to perceive it. The patient inspection of a picture reveals both the historical contingency of human existence as well as the polyvalence of the visual. As the photographer and writer Péter Nádas puts it, there is a mysterious line separating a photograph's corporeal being from its metaphysics.

Pictures tell their stories with ambience, while numbers operate more soberly. Statistics suggest the scale of the passage across the ocean, they tell us where immigrants came from, and where they were going. But while statistics can provide us with numbers, places of origin and destinations for Swiss emigrants to the U.S., they can scarcely explain the complexity of people's lived reality, to say nothing of their desires, their motivations, their ambitions and the material conditions of their lives. This is why we have devoted the most space below to selected biographies and individual stories of migration, featuring both well-known and lesser-known figures. The picture is completed by a series of brief biographical sketches and five portraits. Finally, we wondered why we should confine ourselves uniquely to the Swiss angle; after all, we thought, it would be worth looking at it the other way round as well, and asking what had moved Americans to immi-

grate to Switzerland, and what their impressions have been. Taken together, this variety of representations and perspectives constitutes a panoramic view of Swiss emigration to the U.S., and vice versa. Our choice of subjects makes clear what a diverse set of influences Swiss immigrants have exerted on American life, in the fields of politics, business, technology, entertainment, sports and lifestyle, as well as how persistent this impact has been over the centuries, and down to the present day.

Remember, this story is far from over. People continue to move around the world; immigrants help to form our understanding of our own culture; they are a part of our society, and they will be forever. One of the aims of this book is to remind its readers of this fact, with a range of examples from several centuries. The immigration debate rages on in the U.S. in 2006. Is this still a land of immigrants; does it still want to be a land of immigrants? The economic reality of the United States includes countless clandestine immigrants living outside the law. For its part, Switzerland is in the midst of considering the increasing numbers of asylum-seekers and economic immigrants arriving within its borders, and would do well to remember its own history. "It might be salutary for the immigration debate here if people knew that Switzerland itself was once a land from which people emigrated," says Melissa Auf der Maur, a Canadian singer with Swiss roots who lives in the U.S. "Nobody believes it when I tell them that my grandparents couldn't make a living as cheesemakers in Switzerland. Everyone inevitably thinks that Switzerland has always been rich. But it was poverty that caused my grandparents to leave the canton of Schwyz for North America in 1929." Maybe if Switzerland could remember that it was once a land of emigrants, it might finally realize that it has long since become a land of immigrants.

Illustrations

P.16 Swiss hoping to emigrate overseas assemble with their baggage at the departure camp in Büren am Albis (undated photograph).

P.20 (above) All candidates for immigration to the United States had to stop at Ellis Island. "Undesirables" were detained on the Island until the next ship sailed (undated photograph).

P.20 (below) Immigrants to the U.S. landing at Ellis Island, c.1900. They head for the Processing Center, each carrying a paper with an entry number which they hope to trade for a visa. Ellis Island served as the main immigration point for the U.S. from 1892–1943, processing some 20 million immigrants.

P.21 Women undergo a medical examination on Ellis Island, 1914.

P.23 A Swiss couple, hoping to emigrate overseas, arrives with baggage at the departure camp in Büren am Albis (undated photograph).

P.25 (above and below) Swiss farmers emigrate overseas, 1979.

P.26 The Swiss Athletic Society of Los Angeles is welcomed at Zurich Airport in Kloten on May 28, 1958, by the yodeler Martheli Mumenthaler and the composer Walter Wild (middle). The Athletic Society was to take part in the Federal Marksmanship Festival in Fribourg and the Federal Yodeling Festival in Olten.

Faith and Tradition
Jakob Amman

It seems improbable – a 17th-century Bernese small farmer and artisan of uncertain identity becoming a main actor in the emergence of a Christian faith community that today flourishes in the United States and in the Canadian province of Ontario. Most readers have probably seen Amish people, perhaps on back-country roads traveling by horse and buggy, or they have encountered their picture in magazines, on television, or in movies such as *Witness:* women, dressed in black, with bonnets, shawls, and aprons; bearded men wearing black trousers held up by suspenders, with black overcoats, broad-brimmed hats, and heavy shoes; and Amish youngsters, similarly attired, like miniature grown-ups. The name Amish derives from the last name of a church elder, Jakob Amman or Ammen (c. 1640–1720), about whom as a person much is uncertain, but whose efforts shaped events between 1693 and 1700 in the Alpine foothills of the Swiss canton of Bern, in the Lièpvre Valley north of Colmar in the Alsace, and in the Zweibrücken region east of Saarbrücken in Germany's Palatinate.

The rise of the Anabaptist congregations

When Amman embarked on his mission in 1693, Anabaptist congregations had endured in Switzerland, the Alsace, and the Palatinate for some 170 years despite periodic persecution by the mainline and state-sanctioned Catholic, Lutheran, and Evangelical-Reformed denominations. The epithet "Anabaptists" used by their opponents meant "re-baptizers" and referred to the fact that the dissenters declared infant baptism not only invalid but sacrilegious, and re-baptized those having undergone the rite as infants. They viewed baptism not as a sacrament, but as a symbolic act of submission to the will of God to be performed by adults after mature reflection and serious preparation. Various baptism-inclined groups had formed in the 1520s as part of the institutional break-up of Western Christendom, and they rejected central teachings of reformers like Martin Luther (1483–1546) in the German city of Wittenberg, Huldrych Zwingli (1484–1531) in Zurich, and, two decades later, John Calvin (1509–1564) in Geneva. Although Anabaptists shared with these Protestant reformers a concern for what they considered biblical authenticity, they believed in free will and viewed the church as a union of the converted and virtuous from which all wayward people were to be banished. They also rejected the sword, that is, war, as a state-sponsored evil and regarded the swearing of oaths, especially those of allegiance as demanded by political authorities, as against God's command.

By the mid-16th century, three main Anabaptist groupings had formed, united by their rejection of infant baptism and war but otherwise distinct in doctrine and way of life. In Holland and Northern Germany they were led by men like Melchior Hoffman (c. 1495–1543) and Menno Simons (1496–1561), and came to be called Mennonites after the latter. In rural regions of Switzerland, the Alsace, and the Palatinate, communities formed whose religious convictions were summarized in a communal document known as the Schleitheim Confession after the place of its composition in 1527, a commune in the Swiss canton of Schaffhausen. The document was less a theological exposition than an outline of faith and practice, and its proponents were called

Swiss Brethren and Sisters although communities were forming outside of the Swiss Confederacy as well. A third group became associated with Jakob Hutter (1500–1536), who was preaching in the Tyrolian Puster Valley and whose teaching spread to Moravia. His followers, who came to be named Hutterites, gradually adopted the community of goods and today are settled in northern North America. At times leading members of these Anabaptist groups experienced hardship in the form of heavy fines, expropriations, imprisonment, expulsions and execution, while at other times they encountered relative tolerance.

Amman sounds the alarm

In the decades after 1660 a movement called Pietism emerged among Western Christians. Hardened denominational forms of belief and ritual began to soften under its impact as it influenced most religious groups. Rather than accuracy of belief, the Pietist movement stressed religious experience and virtuous conduct. Lay study and interpretation of scripture were promoted, which began to challenge the doctrinal authority of the established clergy, while private gatherings competed with official church services. Baptism-inclined communities were not immune to these developments. It appeared to Jakob Amman and like-minded associates that soon each minister would have his own view about central tenets of the faith, and in February of 1693 Amman decided to stand against what he considered to be the internal dissolution of belief and practice in the Swiss Brethren congregations. In a sternly worded missive he summoned "all, be they women or men, ministers or common disciples, to appear and present themselves" and to declare whether they observed three propositions, "the shunning of those banned, the expulsion of liars from the fold, and considering no one saved except by the word of God."

At issue was the very nature of the community of the faithful. In opposition to the mainline denominations, the Swiss Brethren had consistently claimed that the true church was not like a pond containing good fish and bad, but only the gathering of the converted who, after having undergone baptism as a result of mature adult decision, led a godly life in full conformity with biblical commands as understood by the Swiss Brethren tradition. Those that were banned from a congregation, Amman and his associates insisted, had therefore to be shunned in every way, that is in word, food and drink, marital relations, and in all other dealings, in order to keep the congregation free from evil contagion and to help the wayward to change. Furthermore, those who had been publicly proven to have sinned, for instance by telling lies, were to be expelled from the congregation until they had mended their ways, despite having confessed their trespass. Finally, no one should declare – thereby questioning Anabaptism's exclusive path to salvation – that non-Anabaptists could also be saved merely by being "treuherzig," that is, good-hearted, kind and helpful to baptism-inclined people.

A meeting called by a certain Peter Habegger at Frieders-Matt near Bowil in the Emmental is exemplary of similar events elsewhere. Jakob Amman asked Niklaus Mosser whether he or his people claimed salvation for those who were outside the Anabaptist fold. He had never heard about it, Mosser answered, and the matter should be left to God's mercy. When questioned, Niklaus Balz from Habstetten near Bern answered likewise, which Amman found evasive and wrong. Hans Reist, who had rejected Amman's moves at an earlier meeting, declined to follow a third summons and to appear at Frieders-Matt. Despite being implored by members of the congregation, among them by a woman falling to her knees, to stop his testing, Amman persisted, believing that the core of the faith was at stake. He excommunicated Hans Reist as an apostate, sectarian and

seducer of God's people and similarly expelled other ministers. "You should know," Amman declared in response to queries from Brethren in the Palatinate, "that these men have not remained in the teaching of Christ and of his epistle."

A meeting held in the Alsace in March of 1694 was attended by ten Swiss and seven Palatine deputies, and Amman's group hoped that their propositions would be accepted – but to no avail. The Brethren from the Palatinate summoned the Swiss deputies to a separate meeting and insisted that they accept Amman's claims about salvation and the expulsion of known sinners, to which they agreed reluctantly; the split then became permanent. Amman's people lamented that now there were "two peoples" of Swiss Brethren and Sisters, the Amman and the Reist group, later to be known as the Swiss Mennonites. Although by 1700 Jakob Amman and his fellow ministers Ulrich Amman, Isaac Kauffman and Niklaus Augsburger acknowledged that they may have been too rash and unbending in conduct and said that they were willing to accept the ban as punishment, no reconciliation ensued, since they did not see a way to relent as regarded the actual issues at hand. Jakob Amman's later whereabouts and the circumstances of his death have remained matters of conjecture, but the division that resulted from his actions endured.

Why did Jakob Amman embark on his journey of inquiry and expulsion? Historians' views differ. Some consider him a firebrand who began a destructive feud among the Swiss Brethren and Sisters. He may have been a newcomer to the faith, one scholar suggests, and thus displayed the typical radicalism of the convert. Others view Amman's three propositions as doctrinal trifles and his insistence on their acceptance as needlessly divisive. Yet understood in the light of the Swiss Anabaptists' foundational statement of faith, his efforts appear to be an attempt to stem what he believed was a gradual erosion of the Anabaptist faith as stated at Schleitheim: "Now there is nothing other in the world and among all creatures than good and bad, believing and unbelieving, darkness and light, the world and those who are outside the world, the temples of God and the idols, Christ and Belial, and none may have any part in the other." Ecumenical accommodation and the tolerance of sinners within the fold, Amman and his associates believed, had no place among the Swiss Brethren, who needed to be protected by physical shunning, the exclusion of the wayward, and faith in exclusive salvation by the Brethren path. In contrast, Hans Reist's group held that the community could practice ecumenical openness and forbearance of the wayward without damaging its core. However one interprets the events, both sides appear to have been sincerely concerned with upholding the faith as they understood it, and both groups have endured in their separate ways. Both have also continued to wrestle with balancing adaptive demands of the times with faithfulness to the substance of their religious tradition. Jakob Amman is not to be viewed as the founder of the Amish communities of the baptism-inclined, but, along with his associates, merely as a voice meaning to hold the baptism-inclined to the fundamentals of the faith as it had been formulated at Schleitheim in 1527.

From 1700 to about 1850 Amish families moved within Europe to wherever they could find tolerant overlords and affordable land, but only sketchy data exist about their migrations. Some Amish moved to the Netherlands in 1711 and in 1750, others to the German state of Hessen in 1730, to Galicia in 1783 and later from there to Russia, and in 1802 Amish families settled in the environs of Ingolstadt and Munich in Bavaria. By the 1870s, however, Amish no longer formed distinct religious communities in Europe, while those who migrated to North America remained separate from other baptism-inclined communities.

Amish communities in North America

Between 1717 and 1750 about 500 Amish people are estimated to have immigrated to Pennsylvania and, from 1817 to 1861, some 1 500 to the American Midwest, coming directly from Switzerland, the Palatinate and the Alsace as well as from Pennsylvania and neighboring regions. The oldest surviving Amish settlement was established in 1757 in Lancaster County. From 1817 until the Civil War, Amish settled mainly on lands newly taken by the government from American native peoples; later they often replaced non-Amish farmers who had gone elsewhere. After 1940 Amish groups moved in all directions within the United States and established settlements in Mexico in 1943, in Belize in 1965, in Paraguay in 1967, and in British Honduras in 1968, which communities, however, did not last. Today the Amish are concentrated in Pennsylvania and the Midwest. The Indiana counties of Holmes and Wayne numbered in 1984 11 districts, or congregations, Pennsylvania's Lancaster County 77, Indiana's Elkhart and Lagrange Counties 54, and Ohio's Geauga and Trumbull Counties 42. The numbers of Amish grew from 3,700 in 1900 to some 85,000 in 1980 and about 200,000 in 2000.

The Amish experienced major divisions in 1870, 1910 and 1966 due to their varying responses to the use of electricity and new technologies such as the automobile or farm machinery. Evangelicals also attracted certain congregations and thus led to separations. Today there are several Amish groups, among them the Old Order and Wisler Mennonite Church, the Beachy Amish Mennonite Church, the Conservative Mennonite Conference and the Old Order Amish, whose baptized members are estimated at 60,000. These groups differ in their response to technological change and governmental intrusion as do the individual congregations, since there is no central church authority.

In daily life Amish speak English and forms of Pennsylvania Dutch, German with admixtures of Palatine dialect and Germanized English elements, while in services they use older forms of written German. Most Amish are farmers or craftspeople, some have their own small businesses, and most are engaged in occupations related to agriculture, which they practice without power-driven machines. Land is not viewed as a commodity, but as a gift "rented" from God. In communication Amish tend to rely on the spoken word and to eschew written legal formalities. Life is not divided into secular and religious domains, but rather all activity is embedded in the practice of the faith. They do not strive for personal and experienced salvation, but for the well-being of the "Gemeinde," the immediate religious community in which they are members. There is no trained clergy to uphold right doctrine, but the bishop, preacher and deacon of a congregation are in unity with the faithful to preserve the proper "Ordnung," that is the communally agreed upon way of life understood as ordained by God. The core of this Amish religious stance, Donald B. Kraybill notes, is "Gelassenheit," that is, an inner distance to all that happens, be it good or bad, welcome or irksome. This is expressed as simplicity in all things, from dress to building to speech, as well as in a dignified tolerance of actions taken by the outside world, be they good, neutral or harmful. The Amish view themselves as God's little people, chosen to abjure the ways of the world while enduring its constant intrusions, in the form of such things as tourism and governmental regulation.

Amish refuse services such as social security or workers' compensation and reject all forms of violence and revenge, including the death penalty. They reject invasive forms of Western medicine like chemotherapy in favor of natural remedies, which occasionally leads to interventions on the part of social agencies. Since the 1950s the Amish have developed numerous primary schools, which are staffed by unlicensed teachers. State governments, such as those of Iowa and Wisconsin, tried to force Amish children into public schools and imposed fines and jail terms on resisting parents until in 1972 the Supreme Court of the United States freed Amish education from outside interference. Conflicts continue to arise over the treatment of milk intended for sale, over signals on Amish vehicles, and over building codes for schools and homes. The path of the Amish, therefore, remains marked by continued intrusions from the outside world, but, seasoned by centuries of experience, they will rise to meet the challenges.

References

Hostettler, Paul, *The Anabaptist Amman/Ammen Families in the Alpine Foothills of Bern: Their Roots and Migration in the Period 1580 to 1713*, trans. Ann C. Sherwin, Pennsylvania Mennonite Heritage 27, 4 (October 2004), pp. 2–19.

Kraybill, Donald B., *The Riddle of Amish Culture*, revised edition, Baltimore, Maryland 2001.

Roth, John D. (trans. and ed.), *Letters of the Amish Division. A Sourcebook*, second edition, Mennonite Historical Publications, Goshen, Indiana, 2002.

Illustrations
P.28 Pennsylvania's pristine landscape.
P.31 Amish carriage in Pennsylvania.
P.33 A group of Amish girls.

Dreams and Daylight
Christoph von Graffenried (1661–1743)

On May 13, 1709, the Bernese aristocrat Christoph von Graffenried set out in secret from Worb. His plan was to travel by way of London to Carolina, far away in North America, where he would found a colony and become wealthy. He left his wife, his eleven children and his creditors behind in Bern. After three years of mishap and adventure on the very edge of the wilderness, including Graffenried's capture by native people and the near destruction of his colony of Neu-Bern, Graffenried returned home, as he put it in his own defense in 1716, under the same unlucky star as had accompanied him on the outward journey. His debts had grown, he was met with coldness by his family, and his grandee's reputation was tarnished. And nevertheless Graffenried had founded Neu-Bern, the oldest Swiss colony in North America.

High-flown ambitions

The Graffenrieds are an old established Bernese noble house. Christoph von Graffenried's father Anton was the lord of the Worb estate. The grand tour prescribed at the time for a well-born gentleman had sporting young Christoph visiting Heidelberg, Frankfurt, Holland and England, where he disported himself at the court of King Charles II. In Cambridge he acquired the title of a Magister Artium in 1682. But Graffenried's newly acquired taste for luxury prompted his impoverished and thrift-loving father to send him on to Paris, where he was just able to visit Versailles before returning home. After ten years away, he was met in Switzerland with resentment for having spent too much money.

On April 25, 1684, Christoph von Graffenried married Regine Tscharner, with whom he would have eleven children over the next 19 years. Despite his wife's privileged background, the heir to the Worb estate kept a tight control over expenses, since Graffenried's own funds were in short supply. At the age of 30 Graffenried was elected to the Great Council of the Two Hundred, the ruling body of the canton of Bern. Eleven years later he was made governor of the country seat of Iferten, today known as Yverdon. While Bern was pleased with Graffenried's administration of his little fiefdom, he himself was unable to make it pay, and, encumbered by gambling losses, obligations and the bills remaining from his grand tour and wedding, he returned to Bern in 1708 owing enormous sums of money.

There was no help to be expected from his tight-fisted father, so Graffenried began urgently searching for a means to cover his debts. It was at this dark hour that the Bernese patrician Franz Ludwig Michel gave him the idea of founding a Swiss colony in America. Michel had visited America and awoke in Graffenried an enthusiasm for its marvelous landscapes and the opulent silver mines he had discovered there. Michel hoped to join forces with a group of Bernese citizens who had founded a colony of their own in 1705 under the leadership of the apothecary Georg Ritter, and thus make a fortune exploiting natural resources. It was the colony's plan to seek support from the English crown, and they saw a promise of great success in the collaboration of Graffenried, scion of the ruling clans.

On May 13, 1709, Graffenried set off in secret for England. Equipped with start-up capital of 7,200 pounds by Georg Ritter & Cie., the Bernese colonial society, he had begun to make reality of his dream of wealth and adventure. His debts and many children he left to his father's care.

Knowing he could count on the support of Queen Anne, Graffenried purchased property in what is now North Carolina from the English Surveyor-General, John Lawson, and the area, a spit of land at the convergence of the rivers Neuse and Trent, was declared the birthplace of a new colony. As the leader of the project, Graffenried was made an honorary citizen of London, as well as Landgrave of Carolina. Michel and Lawson, familiar with the territory, acted as his advisors. The settlers were to be given land within the colony, free of ground rent for the first five years.

Barely a year after Graffenried's departure from Bern, his son Christoph followed him to London, intending to sail with his father for Carolina together with 150 emigrants, among them 50 Anabaptists expelled by the Bernese. These last, however, were not to make the journey: as soon as they set foot on Dutch soil, the local authorities insisted that they be set free. There was no shortage of German religious refugees in England in 1709, however, and Graffenried decided to take along 650 Protestants from Rhineland-Palatinate.

The party set off in two stages: Lawson sailed with the Germans in 1710, reaching the American coast after a stormy crossing only to be met by pirates; just some 300 passengers survived the journey. For his part, Graffenried, accompanied by his son, arrived with the Bernese in their new homeland safe and sound in July of that same year.

There were serious problems to be dealt with immediately. The Germans were starving, and Graffenried had to borrow money to feed them. And then there was the Tuscarora tribe, with whom relations were tense despite the colonists' efforts at peaceful cohabitation. For all that, however, work on Neu-Bern progressed well in the first year and a half, as farming flourished, cattle fed for free, and every necessary trade was represented. Graffenried was already hoping that his town would become the seat of local government.

But the colony had financial woes. There were no silver mines, Neu-Bern was a long way from producing any sort of profits, and Ritter & Cie., the Bernese entrepreneurs, had their doubts about the colony's feasibility in spite of Graffenried's optimistic reports. He insisted that a venture on such a scale required adequate support, and requested additional moneys – in vain. When the English lords of Carolina also proved unwilling to front him funds, Graffenried's situation grew desperate.

The beginning of the end

September of 1711 saw Neu-Bern on the verge of destruction: Graffenried and Lawson had set out on a reconnaissance mission by boat and, unprepared for hostilities, were attacked and kidnapped by natives. It was the beginning of the Tuscarora Indian War. The two were tried in court, where Lawson was sentenced to death and executed. And while Graffenried was acquitted, he only just managed to survive the ensuing six weeks of captivity. It was only upon the signing of a friendship and neutrality treaty with the natives, and the intercession of the Governor on Graffenried's behalf, that he was set free.

In Graffenried's absence, Neu-Bern was practically razed by the natives, who butchered men, women and children, burned their houses down, and killed or stole their cattle. Half of the Germans, too, had joined up with an English settler. Graffenried blamed the hostilities on defamatory claims that he had intended to take

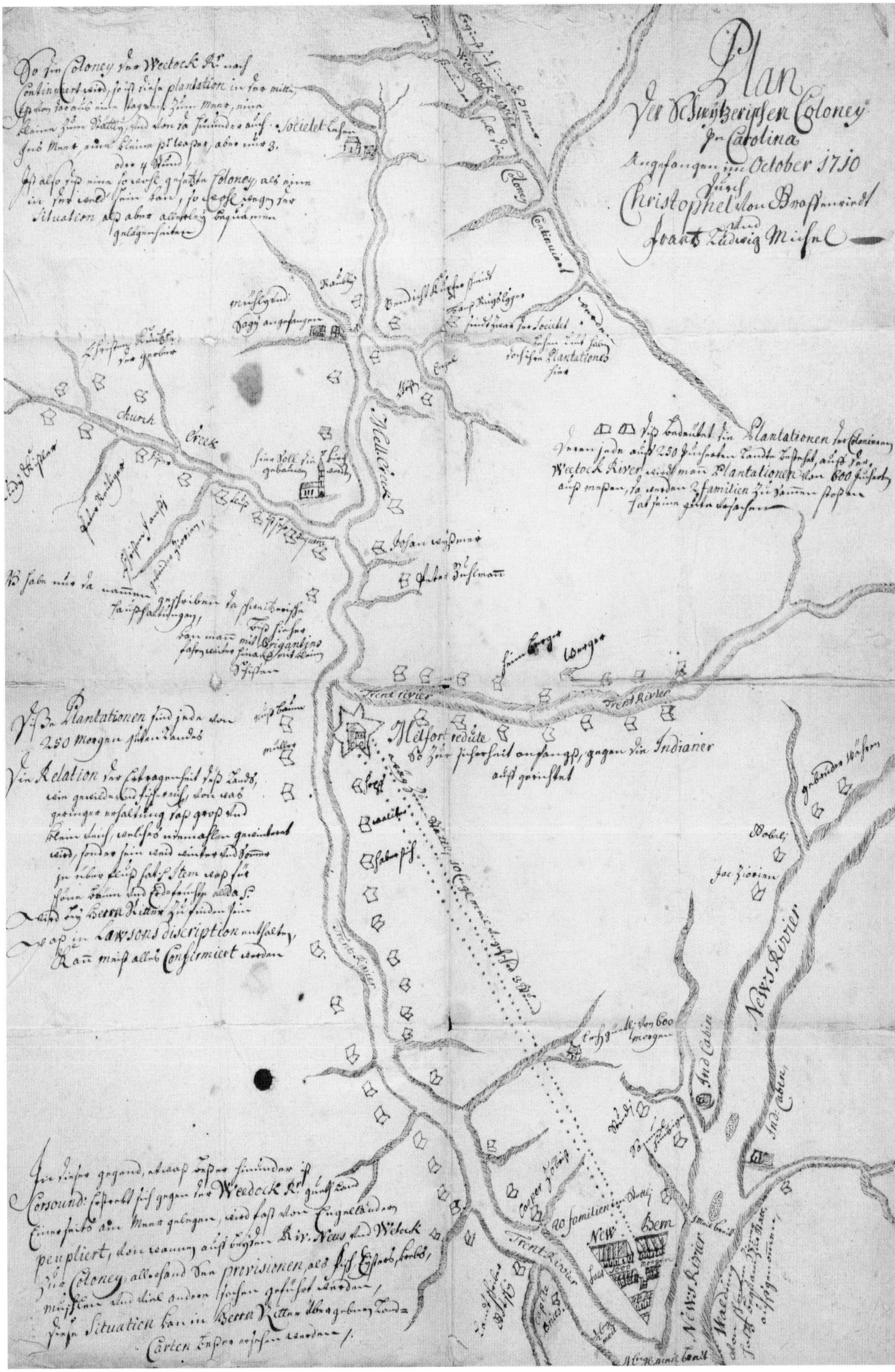

Plan
der Neu-Bernischen Coloney
in Carolina
Angefangen im October 1710
durch
Christophel von Graffenried
und Frantz Ludwig Michel

Weetock River

Mellcira

Church Creek

Melfort redute

Neus River

Trent River

Ind. Cabin

Ind. Cabin

40 familien

NEW BERN

land away from the Tuscaroras, who were definitively conquered in 1713, while also apportioning blame to the Bernese and the neighboring English settlers, whose treatment of the natives had been ruthless.

He went on to attempt to found a colony in Virginia, but was unable to discover any silver mines there either. When at last he was threatened with debtor's prison, Graffenried was advised by the Governor to travel to London and Bern himself to seek a new injection of capital from his backers. He left his beautiful new home reluctantly, knowing that, without money, he would have to "recommend this colony to God's keeping."

Graffenried was unsuccessful at the English court. Indeed, he was immediately pressured by his creditors and was forced to leave the country under a false name. Nor was he welcomed in Bern, where he arrived in early December of 1713. He had been declared bankrupt in absentia, and his father had resigned his seat on the Council for him. Graffenried was obliged to give up his dream of Neu-Bern for good.

In the meantime, Anton von Graffenried had made his grandson Franz Ludwig heir to the Worb estate. Christoph forced his son to renounce the privilege, however, and took over the estate after Anton's death in 1730. This meant the end of his relationship with Franz Ludwig, who in 1734 had himself a new castle built in Worb.

In 1740 Graffenried was made a ward of the state, in order, as the decree noted, to prevent the "utter ruin" of his children and in view of the complaints of misconduct and household mismanagement made against him by his relatives. It was said that, since his father's death, he had amassed more than eleven thousand pounds worth of debt and redeemed certificates that had been deposited for safekeeping. Graffenried died a very old man in 1743.

Reaction in Bern

There is no record of how Graffenried's wife and children reacted to his plans and his secret departure, although it may be assumed that they were not pleased. Barely a year after his son's departure, Anton von Graffenried gave up his seat on the Council. The Bernese did not expect him to return; indeed, they thought his family would follow him to America. Graffenried was later to say that he had suffered a "fatal blow" at his father's hands in the form of his "resignation of my place of honor," a move that he called the "beginning of my ruin." His attempts to regain his seat upon his return were in vain.

His Bernese backers' mistrust and reluctance were surely not completely unjustified, given the colonists' teething pains and the lack of quick profits from the silver mines they had imagined they would find. Moreover, Graffenried's reputation had been badly hurt by his secret departure as well as by the bankruptcy his wife had been forced to declare in order to cover his debts. But the coup de grâce to his solvency was no doubt the loss of his seat on the Council.

Graffenried himself blamed his failure on bad luck; in 1716 he claimed that Michel had tricked him, and that Lawson was responsible for the sorry state of Neu-Bern, having insisted that the colony be created on the hottest and least salutary site.

He seems to have smarted for the rest of his days at the curt and haughty reception upon his return to Worb, and wrote: "The worst of it was that, where I had presumed to seek succour and to reconstitute my dilapidated colony, I was turned back, and thus, lacking assistance from my very own society, which had rejected me, I was regrettably forced to abandon the colony."

The significance of Neu-Bern

The founding of Neu-Bern marks the beginning of the Bernese emigration to North America and is of at least symbolic significance for the history of that phenomenon. Among the first Bernese emigrants was Franz Ludwig Michel, whom Graffenried had followed to found Neu-Bern. The rulers of Bern were opposed to the emigration of their subjects and servants and warned those wishing to leave against the "difficult and uncertain journey, perilous to life and limb." On the other hand, they were happy to be rid of such "nettlesome subjects" as Anabaptists and the indigent. Thus on February 25, 1710, the council and citizens of Bern accepted Ritter's offer to take with him both the local poor and those Anabaptists who were due to be expelled from the territory, in return for financing for the journey.

Despite the government's efforts to stem it, the stream of emigrants grew ever stronger until the 1740s. The authorities were guided by two motives in their opposition. For one thing, they had recognized that the reports arriving from America were often drastically exaggerated; for another, typical of their time, they saw that their country's economic might was directly correlated with the size of its population, the contemporary motor of production. They decreed a range of measures designed to curb emigration, including an embargo on information concerning Carolina as well as, in 1734, a directive to all civil servants and municipalities instructing them to prevent their subjects leaving for the territory. In 1742 the Bernese government forbade its population to emigrate to America on pain of loss of citizenship and expropriation. At the same time, however, the Council studied the causes of the movement and took preventive steps.

It was not until the catastrophic harvest of 1816 that major emigration began. In comparison to the two great waves of overseas emigration, for the most part to the U.S. in the early 1850s and 1880s, older movements such as that to Carolina in 1710 were insignificant.

Christoph von Graffenried's colony of Neu-Bern is a milestone in the history of Swiss emigration. Although it took a while for the colony to recover from its devastation by natives and abandonment by Graffenried, it managed to survive, and by the 19th century New Bern, as it was now known, had become a little trading town with a seaport. Today it numbers 23,000 inhabitants and is renowned as the birthplace of Pepsi Cola, which was invented as "Brad's Drink" in a local pharmacy.

And by the way, Graffenried's eldest son remained in America and moved to Williamsburg near New York, where he married and founded a dynasty that continues to this day. Laura Bush, the wife of U.S. President George W. Bush, is a member of the tenth generation of his descendants.

Literature and sources

Keller, Hans Gustav, *Christoph von Graffenried und die Gründung von Neu-Bern in Nord-Carolina,* Bern 1953.

Lerch, Ernst, *Die bernische Auswanderung nach Amerika im 18. Jahrhundert,* Bern 1909.

Todd, Vincent H. (ed.), *Christoph von Graffenried's Account of the Founding of New Bern,* Spartanburg 1973.

Von Mülinen, Wolfgang Friedrich, *Christoph von Graffenried: Landgraf von Carolina, Gründer von Neu-Bern,* Neujahrsblatt des Historischen Verein des Kantons Bern, Bern 1897.

Illustrations

P. 37 "Plan of the Swiss colony in Carolina, founded in October of 1710 by Christoph von Graffenried and Franz Ludwig Michel"

P. 38 Rendering of Christoph von Graffenried and John Lawson in captivity, by von Graffenried himself. Christoph von Graffenried, John Lawson and a black man are bound and seated on the ground, the execcutioner stands before them. To the right, men, women and children dance around the shaman while two natives beat drums. Armed guards keep watch behind the captives, at the far left a war council is in session.

Money and Diplomacy
Albert Gallatin (1761–1849)

When Albert Gallatin arrived in Washington on January 12, 1801, delayed by snow and rain, he did not yet know that he would be charged with directing the financial destiny of the United States for the next 12 years from what was then a dismal provincial hole. "I took good care of myself and arrived without accident and in good health. I have not even got a cold..." Washington "on the whole is dull," he wrote to his wife, "a place that affords neither news nor entertainment ... Everyone is sick of the place."

It was far from clear at his birth in 1761 into Geneva's aristocracy that Albert Gallatin would one day become the U.S. Secretary of the Treasury. The Gallatin family, whose fortune had been made in trade, had stood at the forefront of Genevan society since the 16th century and had consistently furnished the city-state with rulers. Albert Gallatin moved in radical circles as a student, and he might have gone on to have a brilliant career within Geneva's intellectually stimulati ng Calvinist precincts. At 25 he would have inherited a sizable independence (his parents had died when he was nine), and his way in the city would thus have been paved. Instead, Gallatin fled the sclerotic Geneva political system, driven by a youthful taste for adventure, the promise of easy money and his yearning to be free. At the age of 19 he left his hometown for America, "the freest country in the universe," as he put it. A friend of the family, the Landgrave of Hesse-Cassel, was prepared to offer him a military career, but the young Gallatin had been infected by the democracy virus and refused to serve an absolutist "tyrant."

He arrived in the vicinity of Boston in the summer of 1780 with just 400 silver dollars to his name, since he had not yet come into his inheritance. No sooner had he come to America than he became embroiled in the war against England. He was randomly assigned the command of a corps of volunteers, but, as he himself corrected the legend of his military heroism 65 years later, "I never saw the foe." Believing himself a dab hand at commerce, he invested his capital in tea, hoping to exchange it for other consumer staples. But times were hard and trade was stagnant, and the deal came to nothing. After a difficult winter in the wilds of Maine he returned to Boston penniless, having been unable to sell the Indians either sugar or rum. To make ends meet he worked at first as a French tutor before receiving a position at Harvard University.

But a young man with initiative could not be content as a teacher in the land of unlimited opportunity, and in 1782 he set out for the west in the company of a Frenchman. There he fell ill with a new sickness: speculation. He purchased several thousand acres of land in Pennsylvania, intending to found a Swiss colony there. In the process he was forced to go into a certain amount of debt, which must have troubled the well-bred Calvinist in him. "I could hardly have chosen a less profitable investment for my money," he was to say later. He resolved never again to be in debt, and framed his policies as Secretary of the Treasury in accordance with this precept.

Nor was Gallatin any better at farming than he had been at speculating. Rather, what did distinguish him were his political instincts and his flare for public speaking. When the state of Pennsylvania, where he had settled with his wife Sophia Allegre, held a constitutional convention, he was elected a delegate, and, not long after, a member of the State Legislature. Despite his still limited English (he would speak with a French accent for decades to come), his decisive debating style garnered him power and influence. The sudden death of his wife, however, seemed to spell the end of his meteoric rise as a politician. If he had been able to sell up he would have gone home to Geneva. He fell into a deep depression, spent weeks inside his house and stopped getting dressed. And yet remain he did.

Gallatin expanded his network of acquaintances and returned to Pennsylvania public life, and at the age of 32 was rewarded with election to the United States Senate. At virtually the same time he married Hannah Nicholson, a member of one of New York's leading families with whom he was to have two sons and four daughters. The union catapulted him several rungs up the social ladder. But Gallatin was uncertain whether his election to the Senate had been correct, since he had only been an American citizen for a few months. His political foes shared his doubts and made the most of the scandal, forcing him to withdraw after a year. Just one year later, however, he returned to Washington as a Representative and founded the Standing Committee on Finance, the forerunner of today's Ways and Means Committee.

A voice of reason during the Whiskey Rebellion

The union of 13 states was even then looking for new sources of financing, and in 1791 the federal government decided to levy a tax on the whiskey distilled by farmers from their surplus grain. Over the objections of the farmers, who could not understand why they should be taxed on this product, the federal government pressed on, eager not only for funds but also for an enlargement of its power base. The farmers were outraged and did not beat around the bush: they took up arms, burned down the home of the chief tax collector, tarred and feathered several of his agents, and refused to pay the hated toll. Gallatin emerged as the spokesman of the protesting farmers while at the same time calling for moderation. When hotheads fanned the flames, however, the federal government began to look upon Gallatin as a rebel as well. Although his name appeared on a wanted list he managed to avoid being arrested. His role in the rebellion had no further consequences for him; nevertheless, he was to call it his "only political sin," and his enemies were to hold his participation in the Whiskey Rebellion against him to the end of his days.

President George Washington ordered the Governor of Pennsylvania to send the militia in against the tax dodgers. When the Governor refused to obey, Washington mobilized an army of 13,000 under his own command, the first and only time that a President was to do so. The government had a lot at stake. Had the tax rebels succeeded, it might have led to the collapse of the union and to the emergence of 13 independent states. Gallatin was able to bring calm to this overheated atmosphere. While he continued to find the tax unjust, he thought it more important to avoid a bloodbath; after all, what was taking place was the largest armed conflict among Americans between the Revolution in 1776 and the Civil War in the 1860s.

When the Whiskey Rebellion had come to a peaceful conclusion, due in no small measure to his intercession, Gallatin went back to his career in the House of Representatives, where he gained a reputation for political prowess and became one of the country's leading lawmakers. The first thing he did was subject Alexander Hamilton's Treasury to a review and the obligation to submit an annual report, which won him his colleague's enmity. The two men could hardly have been less alike: while Hamilton ran up debts to finance projects, Gallatin was later to devote himself with an almost manic energy to the reduction of the state deficit.

The greatest real estate deal of all time

Thomas Jefferson was elected President in 1801. The new Chief Executive had been Ambassador in Paris in the 1780s and knew Gallatin's family in Geneva, and it was no doubt due to this connection, as well as to Gallatin's solid financial background, that Jefferson appointed him Secretary of the Treasury. Prior to his appointment Gallatin said that he was being obliged to take upon himself something he had neither sought not desired. He would not have been disappointed if he had not been chosen, he said, filled as he was with doubt as to his own aptitude for the job at hand.

Gallatin, whose first act was to introduce a proper budget process, reckoned that he had been appointed mainly to reduce public debt. And, thanks to his success at this endeavor, Gallatin was able to finance the greatest real estate deal of all time. The Louisiana Purchase was not only the largest property transaction, it was also the most lucrative. The U.S. paid something like $0.3 per acre, later selling off parcels to private settlers to finance the original purchase, a tactic Pennsylvania had employed in the past to fill its own coffers.

As a result, the U.S. acquired a territory of more than half a billion acres without actually intending to. Originally, President Jefferson had wanted to buy only New Orleans from the French, and thus win control of shipping on the Mississippi. He was not interested in the hinterland. Napoleon, too, was initially prepared to part merely with New Orleans before realizing that his European campaigns had drained his resources. The American negotiators, James Monroe and Robert Livingstone, saw for themselves just how desperate his plight was when Napoleon offered them the enormous territory – a quarter of the area of the U.S. today – for a mere pittance, $15,000,000.

As for Gallatin, his financing of the deal was a double coup. On the one hand he had reduced the deficit to the extent that the purchase would not punch a hole in the state's coffers. At the same time, the U.S. was obliged

to send only $11,250,000 to France, the remaining $3,750,000 being set off against claims by U.S. citizens on the French navy, which had been plundering American craft. The U.S. was able to close the deal without raising taxes, another reason for Jefferson's re-election.

Peacemaker and ethnologist

After some years at the Treasury Gallatin seemed to be nearing his goal of eradicating the federal deficit. And yet the threat of a civil war, a trade embargo, the coming war in Europe and extraordinary expenses of which he did not approve were making his life difficult. Without actually resigning he took time off, as it were, to act as a broker in the war Congress had declared against England in 1812. At issue were both territorial disputes and the American circumvention of the British trade embargo against France. The differences came to a head in 1812 with violent skirmishes, and the British even marched on Washington, burning down Gallatin's house in the process. Gallatin himself was not at home, but someone from within his residence had fired on the British, who returned the volley.

The peace talks were tricky, the parties to the conflict unbending. Gallatin traveled to Russia, which had offered its assistance with the negotiations. Finally, on December 24, 1814, the opponents signed the Treaty of Ghent, ending the war with England. Gallatin wrote of the conflict: "The war has strengthened the national sentiment. The people are now more American; they feel and act as a nation, and I hope that the nation has become as a result more secure."

The Treaty of Ghent is considered one of Gallatin's greatest feats of diplomacy, and he stepped down as Secretary of the Treasury that same year, having reduced the deficit by about half. The accomplishments of his term in office include the construction of the marine hospitals, the predecessors of today's health administration. He also encouraged the creation of a road joining east and west, today's U.S. Route 40. The state financed the construction, and the first section was inaugurated in 1818.

After making peace in Ghent, Gallatin took the opportunity to visit his hometown of Geneva after 35 years of absence. Only a few of his relatives were still alive. From Geneva he stopped off in Paris, where he met Napoleon, who had returned from exile on Elba and was briefly in ascension again. The following period, 1816–1823, Gallatin spent as Ambassador to France and England. This called for little diplomacy but plenty of social life, which he greatly enjoyed.

In 1830 Gallatin fulfilled a long-held wish, the "establishment of a general system of rational and practical education fitted for all, and gratuitously open to all." There was a great desire for a university in New York, particularly one that could satisfy the growing demand for well-educated people. A group of more than a hundred figures from the arts and sciences gathered in October of that year in a founders' assembly and voted Gallatin the first President of New York University. He remained only a few months in that office, however, since religious zealots took over the institution and turned it away from Gallatin's original liberal principles.

Gallatin had two sides: he was a scrupulous number-cruncher, spending nights buried in the confusing details of the federal budget while Secretary of the Treasury. Upon withdrawing from politics he returned to the world of finance, founding the National Bank of the City of New York. But it was his own financial need that led to him becoming President of the bank at the age of 70, as decades of underpaid public service had shrunk his reserves and his real estate speculation had come to nothing.

More than banking, however, it was the study of the culture and language of the native peoples that consumed him during the final decades of his life. With the same energy that had characterized his work with the state's finances, he thoroughly researched the peculiarities of the native tongues until his death in 1849. He founded the American Ethnological Society and published a series of carefully researched studies, and is known in certain circles as the father of American ethnology. His attitude to the native peoples was informed by a call for assimilation with the American settlers. He himself esteemed the books he wrote about native cultures more highly than his works on financial policy, which were standards for decades.

Albert Gallatin was buried quietly in New York during a cholera epidemic in 1849 that had emptied the city. He had been confined to his bed for almost a year and died in the arms of his daughter Frances, three months after the death of his wife. Certain of his principles remain valid today, 150 years later. He was for instance a great believer in the necessity of a strong government and healthy finances. He was a liberal for whom the state was not an enemy power but rather the guarantor of personal liberty. He was a champion not only of American interests but was a "citizen of the world," according to his biographer, John Austin Stevens. Together with his earlier predecessor, Alexander Hamilton, Gallatin is considered one of the pre-eminent Treasury Secretaries in the history of the United States. Hamilton was a genius at organizing the financial system of the still young republic, while it was Gallatin's accomplishment to halve the deficit. He brought "typically Swiss" qualities to the Treasury: he was reserved, balanced in judgment, honest and modest. What he lacked, however, were the very characteristics needed in the burgeoning state – bravery, decisiveness and vision.

Literature

Adams, Henry, *Life of Albert Gallatin,* Philadelphia 1879.

Boxall Jr., James A., *Albert Gallatin and American Foreign Policy: A Study in Thought and Action,* dissertation Michigan State University 1967.

Kuppenheimer, L. B., *Albert Gallatin's Vision of Democratic Stability,* Westport 1996.

Stevens, John Austin, *Albert Gallatin: An American Statesman,* Boston/New York 1883.

Illustrations

P. 43 Painting of British and American delegates meeting to sign the Treaty of Ghent (1814). Gallatin is sixth from left.

P. 44 $ 500 dollar bill bearing the likeness of Albert Gallatin, in circulation from 1862–1863.

P. 45 The statue of Albert Gallatin in front of the U.S. Treasury Building in Washington, DC.

Bernard R. Bachmann

Rise and Fall

Johann August Sutter (1803–1880)

Every life history is composed of facts, events and documentation. But it is also a matter for subjective judgment, at the mercy of contemporary ideological conceptions. For this reason, there are several different versions of each biography: the factual curriculum vitae, the hagiography (as has long been Sutter's case), and the sober interpretation.

The facts

Sutter was born in 1803 in Kandern, in southern Germany, where his Swiss father was the director of the local paper mill. His mother was a pastor's daughter. Sutter spent his childhood and school days in Kandern before going on to an apprenticeship with Thurneysen publishers and booksellers in Basel. When he had completed this practical training he worked from 1823 to 1824 in Aarburg as a clothier's clerk. It was here that he met Annette Dübeld, the daughter of the widow of a wealthy Burgdorf baker and innkeeper, and the couple was married on October 24, 1826, in Burgdorf. Johann August junior was born the next day.

Four more children came in short order. Sutter worked for a few years for the salt merchant Aeschlimann before receiving the permit he required as a non-local to open his own haberdashery. But the business was short-lived, declaring bankruptcy in 1834. Sutter emigrated via Le Havre to New York, leaving behind his wife, their five young children – and a mountain of debt: he owed more than 51,000 Swiss francs, which today would amount to well over half a million dollars.

He stayed in New York only briefly before going to St. Louis, the center of German-speaking immigration, and trying his hand at the Santa Fe trade. He moved on to California in 1838, reaching it in 1839 after detours via Oregon, Hawaii and Russian America (Alaska). At the time California was still a province of Mexico, and the Governor gave him some 50,000 acres on the Sacramento River, on the site of what would one day be the city of Sacramento. Later, as a token of thanks for his help in putting down a revolt, Sutter was to receive a second gift of land.

Sutter founded New Helvetia and built Sutter's Fort. But the colony suffered alternately from drought and flooding, as well as from a lack of trustworthy and experienced workers, and when Sutter purchased Fort Ross in Russian America with New Helvetia as collateral, the mortgage was simply more than could be borne.

In the meantime, California had become a part of the U.S., having been occupied by the Americans in 1847 during their 1846–1848 war with Mexico. By the terms of the Treaty of Guadalupe Hidalgo (signed in January of 1848), Mexico ceded the entire area of what is now the southwestern United States, including California, to the young republic. The change of government and the development of a functioning American administration were a slow and chaotic process, with communication between Washington, DC, and the west coast taking four to six months by land and up to nine months by sea.

In early 1848, at around the same time as the state was changing hands, James Marshall struck gold while leading an expedition to the Sierra Nevada to set up a sawmill for Sutter. The notorious California Gold Rush had begun. Within three years, the population of California had grown from between three and five thousand to several hundred thousand.

Sutter was now a rich man, able to pay off the debts incurred in the Russian-American purchase. He held onto New Helvetia and Sutter's Fort (the germ of present-day Sacramento), which were to become the headquarters of the several hundred thousand gold-diggers arriving from all over the world.

But the Gold Rush was a roller coaster, and in a few years Sutter had lost everything, his trusty employees, his cattle, his property, even his second Mexican land grant, taken from him by the U.S. Supreme Court after years of legal wrangling. Nor did he have any luck running for the governorship of California, although he just narrowly missed being elected as one of Arnie's predecessors. Resigned to his fate, Sutter retired to his Hock Farm estate to become what his peers had long held him to be, a California pioneer, farming and establishing orchards and vineyards.

In 1865 his house burned down, probably an act of arson following the firing of a worker. Nothing kept Sutter in California now, and he set out for home. His return journey to Switzerland was interrupted by a stop-over in Washington, where he sought reparations from the Congress for the damages he had sustained during the heady days of the Gold Rush – but to no avail, and he died, a disappointed failure, in 1880.

The hagiography

The saga of Sutter as hero began to be told while he was still alive. According to this account, his was a personality that could not be contained within the narrow confines of Restoration-era Switzerland, and he set out to create something new on a faraway, foreign continent, at great risk to life and limb.

Forced by circumstances beyond his control to leave his homeland, he picked himself up and in a spirit of daring entrepreneurship braved the odds at the end of the world, the American west coast. Many of those he met along the way were impressed by his background and bearing, and attest to his ability, his foresight and his trustworthiness.

He showed the lazy descendants of the Spanish conquerors how to till the land and live by it, the legend goes, and he made allies of the savage, thieving Indians of California's interior. He harnessed them in his project of taming the wilderness and thus freed them from the petrified state in which the Spanish missions had left them when they disbanded.

He was robbed of the fruits of his labors by hordes of greedy, lawless prospectors, before whom even the American lawmakers capitulated as they invaded California in their hundreds and thousands, and stole the greater part of his land.

The source of this version is to be found in Sutter's own autobiography, itself a collection of many slight variations on the theme. His memoirs, along with his voluminous correspondence, are a congeries of invention, omission, embellishment and deliberate self-representation as a victim. They include the fiction of his having served as an officer in the French army and notably exclude some less than glorious episodes, such as his bankruptcy in Burgdorf and his abandonment of his family. Sutter either passes over or downplays his shameful treatment of native people, especially his dastardly way with indigenous women both on the continent and in Hawaii, as well as his career as a spendthrift and debtor.

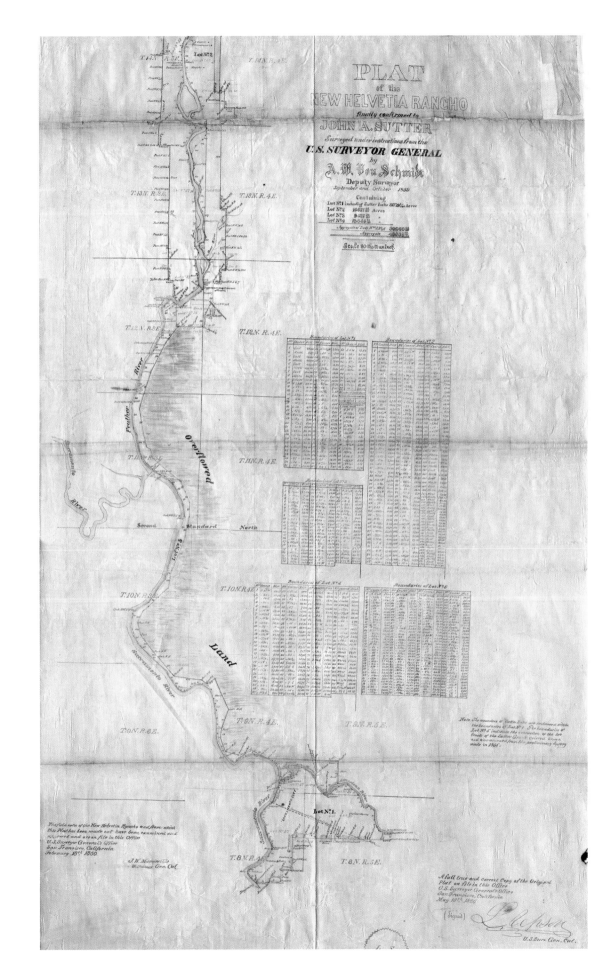

PLAT
of the
NEW HELVETIA RANCHO
finally confirmed to
JOHN A. SUTTER
Surveyed under instructions from the
U.S. SURVEYOR GENERAL
by
A. W. Von Schmidt
Deputy Surveyor
September and October 1859

Containing
Lot Nº1 including Sutter Lake 8879¼ Acres
Lot Nº2 16637½ Acres
Lot Nº3 9457½
Lot Nº4 15449¼

Scale 80 chs to an inch.

He sees himself as the victim whenever things do not turn out as he had planned, and is evidently incapable of drawing a connection between his own behavior and actions and their results. This Sutter spends his life advancing, fleeing the devastation he has wrought, never looking back, never looking within himself.

Sutter's self-beatification was adopted by his first biographers, to culminate in such works as Blaise Cendrars's *Gold* and **Stefan Zweig's** *El Dorado.*

But the hagiography cannot have been based solely on Sutter's own accounts, for without the myth of the frontier in general, he would have remained an anecdotal footnote to the chronicle of California, or disappeared altogether into the dustbin of history.

This myth was crucial over the course of more than a century as the west was won and an American self-image was developed. The frontier is the imaginary dividing line between the east, the settled areas of North America, and the proverbial Wild West.

During the 19th century and with enormous physical effort, this line was moved successively westward by countless immigrants, mostly from Europe, until it came to a natural end at the Pacific. These were the pioneers. The myth of the frontier had the following central components: a supposedly untouched wilderness and a free country, heroic masculinity and the overcoming of terrific dangers. Sutter was a prominent exemplar of this generation of American pioneers. His role as the first person to settle and cultivate the wilds of California was that of a hero, the hero of an entire generation. He was the embodiment of the frontier spirit and a permanent figure in its mythology.

The interpretation

It is clear from his history that Sutter was a lousy businessman and an even worse judge of character. He was always biting off more than he could chew, forever joining forces with business partners who shamelessly took advantage of his naivety and lack of experience to hoodwink him.

His life is filled with unexplained, indeed inexplicable gaps. He learned the bookseller's trade, but his master did not hire him, so he moved to another canton (no mean feat in 1823) and changed his profession. Two years later he had an illegitimate child underway and another new environment, but, despite the financial ease afforded eventually by a well-to-do mother-in-law, he managed within a matter of years to amass enormous debts. In St. Louis and on the Santa Fe trail he made more enemies and was forced to flee. Instead of settling in Oregon, however, his stated purpose, he ran up further debts in Fort Vancouver, where he had been hospitably entertained, as well as, later, in Hawaii. New Helvetia, too, lived constantly under the threat of collection and bankruptcy.

Sutter was a dreamer and an enthusiast. As an apprentice he had come to love reading, and the records of his bankruptcy proceedings in Burgdorf show that he used to buy books, costly books. He had probably come across **Gottfried Duden's** *Bericht über eine Reise nach den westlichen Staaten Nordamerikas und einen mehrjährigen Aufenthalt am Missouri* (Report of a journey to the western states of North America and several years' sojourn on the Missouri), which the Swiss emigrants' society had reissued in 1832. Emigration was in the air in the 19th century. Many Swiss became economic refugees; many departed willingly, while others were "outsourced" by their communities, which chartered ships for entire groups and sent the troublesome citizens off into the world with a bit of money.

Sutter was not a typical Swiss emigrant, being neither politically nor religiously persecuted. He was an outlaw, preferring (quite understandably) to flee his debts than to languish as a failure.

He knew exactly where he wanted to go: Missouri. He just didn't know what he wanted to do there, or what awaited him upon his arrival. He did know what he could not expect: a social safety net, consular aid and the security that comes of being part of a group of like-minded fellows. He knew he was on his own. And yet he went, since the risks and the uncertainty of the New World were less awful than his prospects in Switzerland. He could probably see the financial ruin of his Burgdorf business coming. After his departure it was determined that books, clothing and even money listed on his inventory were missing. He had evidently planned his escape. He could never have managed the journey to Le Havre, the crossing to New York and the months of travel to St. Louis without means, and he needed start-up capital for his Santa Fe venture.

He must have hoped that his Swiss bankruptcy had been a one-time thing, that he would make it big in America and be able to pay off his debts. Wishful thinking like this seems to have been his modus operandi. But he fell into a vicious circle of ambition, failure and escape. The Gold Rush was his big chance, his one opportunity to break out of this circle – and he muffed it. His eldest son arrived in California just in time for the Gold Rush, and Sutter handed on his business to him. Together with a dependable and experienced overseer, young Sutter managed to get New Helvetia's affairs in order. He paid off the debts incurred in Burgdorf, in Russian America and with New Helvetia's many suppliers. Prudent, clever and cautious, the Sutters were now able to exploit the Gold Rush and become one of the richest families in the world. But it was not to be: while his son was whipping his affairs into shape with the future first Governor of California, Sutter was having fun with the prospectors, throwing lavish parties and playing the big hero. Back in Sacramento he fired his son and advisor, fell into the clutches of ruthless connivers, speculated away his best and most valuable properties, and literally lost everything.

In the end, Sutter was himself to blame for his financial undoing. It required neither thieving gold-diggers, illegal settlers nor the loss of his two Mexican land grants to deliver the coup de grâce. His Gold Rush, a failure of discipline, character, dependability and wit, was proof that he was not a born businessman. He was an opportunist, a dilettante and a lightweight. At the same time, however, he was also a charmer, a bold "entrepreneur" willing to take risks, someone who could see an opportunity and was ready to make the most of it. In the end he failed because he lived beyond his means, forever making empty boasts and never thinking through – or completing – what he had embarked on.

Literature and sources

Bachmann, Bernard R., *General J. A. Sutter: Ein Leben auf der Flucht nach vorn,* Zurich 2005.

Zollinger, James Peter, *Johann August Sutter: Der König von Neu-Helvetien; sein Leben und sein Reich,* Zurich 2003.

Neu-Helvetien – Lebenserinnerungen des Generals Johann August Sutter, retold from manuscripts edited by Erwin Gustav Gudde, Verlag Huber & Co. Aktiengesellschaft, 1934.

Illustrations

P. 49 Map of New Helvetia, 1859.

P. 50 Californian prospectors panning for gold, 1849.

P. 51 Portrait of Johann August Sutter by Frank Buchser, 1866.

Socialism and Utopia
Andreas Dietsch (1807–1845)

What can you write about a man who left nothing more than a few notes on his utopian vision of a better world, and whose attempt at putting that vision into practice in the wide-open spaces of the Midwest is today commemorated by a rusty pair of scissors, a single apple tree and a few graves? What is one to say?

What you can do is credit Andreas Dietsch, who left the canton of Argovia for North America during the summer of 1844 in the company of just 42 would-be emigrants, with actually attempting to do what other people only dreamed about: found a society free of greed and envy, a community based on common property whose members all enjoy the same rights and live in freedom together. Here is the relevant passage from the articles of association for the emigrant society formed by Dietsch: "This colony [to be established in America] shall forever abolish the ancient ills which have oppressed humanity for thousands of years now and are to blame for its present condition, in which the toiling classes are delivered to contempt and deprivation, and those with wealth or quality of birth are given sway over their fellows. This colony shall therefore be a confraternity after the teachings of Jesus Christ, with no estate and no lineage enjoying any advantage over any other. ... And to completely stifle usury and profit-seeking and stanch such dangerous desires, the colony shall forbid its members to make use of money among themselves, reserving currency solely for trade with the outside world. ... The colony of New Helvetia shall be for all time an indivisible and inviolable commonwealth, in which every member shall have the same rights and the same share of use, profit and loss, without exception granted for estate, guild or lineage."

When they set out to make this vision a reality, Dietsch and his companions accepted the possibility of failure; and indeed, the colony of New Helvetia in the American state of Missouri was not destined to endure. Dietsch seems to have understood this towards the end of his life, which was also the end of the colony.

"It pains my soul," he wrote to a correspondent in Switzerland a few months before his death, "that I cannot relate to you the fulfilment of all the wonderful things we hoped to accomplish in our new homeland; ... it is the most difficult of all labors to begin and to execute any plan together with people of various sensibilities. ... I have been scrupulous in not omitting anything from my reports to you, so that neither I nor the others may be charged with attempting to deceive you. Our failing has not been that of will, but rather must be laid at the feet of our ignorance; we are now forced to admit that our comprehension was imperfect, for each relied too heavily on the others."

The fascination of utopias

Anton Andreas Dietsch, or Andres Dietsch, as he called himself, was born in October 13, 1807, in Mülhausen (the town had until 1798 a contractual relationship with the Swiss Confederation), today Mulhouse in the Alsace region of France. Dietsch's schooling was by his own account quite inadequate, and he was forced to combat the poverty in which his family lived by taking up a trade, that of a humble brush maker, at an early age. In 1831 he had himself registered as a journeyman and took to the road. Where exactly he went can no longer be reconstructed, but we next pick up his traces in 1835 in Aarau, where the town council granted him a residence permit as an apprentice to the brush maker Gabriel Hagnauer. One year later, the cantonal government of Argovia approved his marriage to Hagnauer's daughter. The couple lived from 1836 to 1838 in Zofingen, then moved to Aarau, where Dietsch opened his own business as a purveyor of brushes. His wife died in 1843 shortly after the birth of their third child, a son, who lived for only seven days. Dietsch was now left to care for his two daughters alone.

His first work, a pamphlet entitled *Der Aarauer Bachfischet* published in 1841, takes its name from a medieval custom, still practiced annually today, involving cleaning out the local brook. It is an early testament to the utopian socialism that would preoccupy him later on. The text is a meditation on the mores and social inequities of the age, with special attention to the plight of tradesmen in the burgeoning industrial era, suffering under the flood of cheap foreign imports. It was becoming increasingly expensive to feed oneself and acquire the materials necessary for one's trade, he wrote, while at the same time one's prices could not be raised to take account of the inflation; indeed, they were dropping year by year. It was impossible to get ahead as an honest craftsman, and the field was being abandoned to those willing to cheat and keep their eye firmly on the main chance. As Dietsch was later to write elsewhere, all he demanded for himself and his kin was shelter, food and clothing. This was his most sacred due as a citizen of the world, he maintained, one who toiled in the service of the common good.

It was thus no wonder that the author of such screeds should also write for the *Posthörnchen,* an Argovian weekly known for its unvarnished liberal critique. Between 1841 and 1843, the *Posthörnchen* published more than 50 pieces of social criticism by Dietsch, written for the most part in the local dialect. He was not the only one of his contemporaries to speak out against the prevailing regime, in which the poor were thrust ever deeper into misery and the oppressed kicked when they were down, while the ruling classes profited from the situation. In Zofingen his prominent comrades-in-arms were the physician and social reformer Rudolf Sutermeister and the manufacturer Gustav Siegfried, the latter of whom leaned towards socialism. Sutermeister was an admirer of the novel *Voyage en Icarie* (1840) by the French utopian socialist Etienne Cabet, with its description of a perfect worker's state guided by the utter commitment to equality and common property. The doctor was able to persuade Dietsch himself to compose a "romantic account of a communal economy," *Das Tausendjährige Reich* (The 1000-year dominion, 1842), which first appeared in the *Posthörnchen.*

Dietsch begins with a sketch of a suffering society and the causes of its misery, greed and overweening ambition, which have divided its members into rich and poor, ruler and ruled. This analysis is followed by an appeal to the wealthy – indeed, to all of humanity – to come to their senses and discover their fellow feeling, and concludes with a vision of a paradise of complete human freedom and equality, in which labor is performed with joy and without compulsion and all receive their basic due. Considered in its wider context, Dietsch's is merely one of many contemporary utopias being imagined as a response to the so-called "social question."

The dream of New Helvetia

The apathetic public reception of Dietsch's text proved that his vision of an egalitarian community with property held in common was not feasible in Switzerland. Undaunted, Dietsch soon began to think more practically and, in **December 1843, published a third piece,** *Die Gründung von Neuhelvetia, ein sicherer Wegweiser für Auswanderungslustige, welche in Amerika ihr Glück suchen und begründen wollen* **(The founding of New Helvetia, a trusty guide for would-be emigrants seeking to establish their fortune in America). This book met with un-qualified success and led to such a slew of queries and applications that Dietsch was nearly overwhelmed as he tried to respond to them all.**

A project of emigration like Dietsch's must also be seen against the backdrop of European imperial expan-sion in the 19th and 20th centuries, characterized as it was by mass movements of people. Between 1850 and 1930, more than 50 million Europeans went overseas, including some 330,000 from Switzerland; a significant share of these emigrants settled in North America. There were multiple reasons for the exodus, among them poor harvests, destitution and the resulting lack of confidence in the economic future of one's home country, along with a profusion of exuberant reports from those who had already made the voyage. Nor was emigra-tion by any means always voluntary. Many communities sought to rid themselves once and for all of their responsibilities to their indigent members by paying the costs of their expatriation, reasoning that this was certainly cheaper than supporting them indefinitely.

Dietsch's diary and the log books of his emigrant society were published in Aarau in 1845, giving us a wealth of information about the journey and the first months of his sojourn in Missouri. On June 2, 1844, Dietsch left Aarau with a company of 39; three further emigrants joined them later. Some hundred people saw the trave-lers out of the city. After approximately three weeks' march they reached Le Havre, where they booked their passage and laid in supplies for the lengthy crossing. Finally, on June 26 at 6 in the morning, the *Albany* **set sail from the harbor. All of its passengers were on deck, watching the city grow smaller and the French coast dwindle slowly out of sight. On July 29, following a terrible bout of seasickness that had afflicted him along**

THE IRON STEAMSHIP "GREAT EASTERN" 22,500 TONS.

Constructed under the direction of I. K. Brunel, F.R.S.–D.C.L.

Commanded by Capt. William Harrison.

with almost all of his comrades, Dietsch was once again able to make a more extensive entry in his diary. "Above deck and below, to left and to right, day and night there is a great purging from both ends; all day long the chamber pots are passed back and forth directly below one's nose." All of this, however, was simply "something we all of us must get through, and with a little patience it will come out all right in the end."

Around August 1 the ship reached Long Island. The plumb line was cast every quarter of an hour as the craft prepared to dock, the sails were furled and the anchor was let down. After 38 days at sea, the ship was now quarantined across from the hospital. With the customs formalities quickly accomplished, Dietsch and his companions were beset while still on Ellis Island by a swarm of German brokers seeking to sell them further passage into the interior. In the end, however, Dietsch went into the city alone to organize the group's journey on from New York, where he was once again molested by "innkeepers and agents, who importuned me as soon as they learned my name, pulling me to left and to right as if I were heaven knows what... Each tried to steal the new arrivals away from the other; three weeks before we docked it had already been common knowledge that our society was traveling to New York on the *Albany.*"

Finally a deal of sorts was struck for the journey to Pittsburgh, although Dietsch was soon forced to conclude that "one is led on and cozened on all sides here if one does not possess reliable relations or acquaintances with good English and a command of the Americans' trickery, as well as that of the Europeans resident among them." It is interesting to note that the newcomers did in fact have such local acquaintances, indeed that some had relatives locally. In Philadelphia Dietsch visited his brother-in-law, who had been living in the U.S. for 11 years. From there the company continued by water via Pittsburgh and Cincinnati to St. Louis, arriving on September 1, 1844.

Not long after, a small contingent went on to look for a suitable piece of property on which to build New Helvetia. In the end they purchased 360 acres in Osage County, some 7 and a half miles above the spot where the Osage River joins the Missouri in the 20th and 21st sections of *"Taunschipp"* 43. The immigrants moved to the property on September 22 and began to set up their new home.

The end of the colony

Fortune did not smile on the enterprise. The company suffered under the weather and the unfamiliar climate, and as illnesses made the rounds the group was sorely tested by these difficult circumstances. Some were simply not up to it, as Dietsch wrote: "My call for the establishment of New Helvetia and its subsequent statutes were all very well on paper, but it is quite another matter to act upon these and to make good on one's noble intentions. One sits at home and reads such things and imagines how pleasant it must be to live in peace with one another, how easy to work together, to endure and to be stoical; but in the event reality is quite different. ... Envy, personal dislike and selfishness have loosened the bonds of union and our striving for a handsome future. ... It pains my soul that I cannot relate to you the fulfilment of all the wonderful things we hoped to accomplish in our new homeland..."

The colony began to disband in the spring of 1845. The means and causes of this dissolution are not known, nor do we have any details of Dietsch's death sometime during that same season. Some of the remaining New Helvetians helped to found a community in Iowa in 1847, in some ways the successor to New Helvetia. This too, however, disbanded in the mid-1850s. In the cemetery in Communia, Clayton County, Iowa, the gravestone of Johan (John) Enderes (1812–1892) still stands. It reads, in German, "Joh. Enderis, smith fr. Mümmenhausen, Baden, unmarried," commemorating one of the founders of New Helvetia and a co-signer of the Communia constitution. New Helvetia is now a cow pasture. Decades after the disappearance of the colony, a rusty pair of scissors was found there. Along with a few graves and an apple tree, still standing 70 years ago, it is the only reminder of what once was meant to be a thousand-year dominion.

Literature and sources

Die grossartige Auswanderung des Andreas Dietsch und seiner Gesellschaft nach Amerika, **Zurich 1978.**

Dietsch, Andreas, *Die Gründung von Neu-Helvetia,* **Langenthal 1844.**

Halder, Nold, *Andreas Dietsch und seine Utopistenkolonie Neu-Helvetia in Missouri: Ein Beitrag zur Geschichte der schweizerischen Emigration und des Frühkommunismus in der Schweiz,* **Aarauer Neujahrsblätter special edition 1960 and 1961, Aarau, no date.**

Illustrations

P. 55 Empty landscape in Missouri.

P. 56 Historical illustration showing the Great Eastern, one of the earliest trans-Atlantic passenger liners. The ship, designed by a British engineer, was 656 feet in length and, at the time of its construction, the longest vessel in the world.

Prejudice and Perseverance
Guggenheim & Co.

If one believes the (family) accounts, the story of the Guggenheims is like a fairy tale. It all begins in 1847 with our hero, Simon Guggenheim, as in so many fairy tales a bitterly poor tailor, in the Argovian village of Lengnau. From the late 18th century until 1866, Jews in Switzerland were permitted to settle only here and in the neighboring village of Endingen. The authorities had been extremely careful to keep down the population of these two communities since the first Jewish families had begun immigrating in the 1600s, denying them citizenship and attaching conditions to their residence permits. Jews had to have their charter (or laissez-passer) renewed every 16 years by the local lord in Baden, and had to pay on occasion the equivalent of a half year's wages for the privilege. If they wished to leave their communities they were subject to a so-called "Judenzoll," a form of polltax. Although excluded from the army, Jews were fined for not doing military service. And, during the 19th century, like all non-citizens or those living in straitened circumstances, Jewish couples required a marriage licence. Would-be wives had to provide a dowry of at least 500 guilders or be turned down for the authorities' approval, a strategy aimed at preventing the communities' having to support the indigent. The two Jewish villages protested against these punitive measures, and in 1866 they were victorious: the Federal Constitution was amended to guarantee equal rights to all Swiss. The members of the Jewish communities of Endingen and Lengnau were at last formally and legally entitled to settle anywhere in Switzerland.

Forbidden to marry

But to get back to Simon Guggenheim. He was born in Lengnau in 1792, the son of Meyer and Vögel Guggenheim. Sometime around 1815 he married Schäfeli Levinger, with whom he had a son and five daughters before her death in 1836. Meyer, their only son, was born in 1828 and did his part for the family upkeep by working as a traveling salesman, dealing in buttons, ribbons, cookware and shoelaces. It was difficult for the poor tailor to come up with the dowry needed to marry off his daughters.

Rachel Weil Meyer, the next character in our saga, was also resident in Lengnau. She was a widow with three sons and four daughters and lived on the modest savings left to her by her late husband. In 1847 Rachel Weil Meyer and Simon Guggenheim made plans to marry and merge their two households, but were denied the necessary permit.

So the pair, intent on marriage, decided to continue their fairy tale elsewhere. In the mid-19th century it was said that there were no restrictions placed on Jews in America, and that they could seek their fortune there and begin a new life. It is unknown how rumors to this effect had made it to Lengnau. Perhaps Meyer Guggenheim had brought them home with him from his travels through Argovia and Southern Germany, or perhaps they came from distant relatives or acquaintances living already as emigrants abroad. However they came to hear of them, Simon Guggenheim and Rachel Weil evidently

believed these accounts of the New World, and the 55-year-old widower and his 41-year-old fiancée decided to sell their houses, pack their belongings, and leave Switzerland for America with their 12 children in
common. From Koblenz the two families traveled down the Rhine by ship and made it eventually to Hamburg,
setting sail from there to Philadelphia, which they reached after a crossing of some three months.

From peddler to millionaire

The United States in 1848 was a turbulent place full of promise. The Gold Rush was just beginning and
had already injected incredible wealth into the economy, while the end of the war with Mexico had brought
stability and new trading partners. At the time, Philadelphia, a center of finance and textiles dominated by
wealthy Christians from Northern Europe, was thought to be the most attractive and tolerant city in America.
The Jewish population of America was some 50,000, 2,500 of whom lived in Philadelphia.

Soon after arriving in their new homeland, Rachel Weil and Simon Guggenheim were finally able to marry.
Simon went on to work with his son Meyer as a peddler, dying at the age of 76 in 1869. Not much more is
known about the life led by Simon Guggenheim and Rachel Weil Meyer in the New World, but the renown of
the family's subsequent generations makes up for this lack. In addition to the usual peddler's items, Meyer
Guggenheim also sold stove polish and coffee essence. Not content, however, with the modest retailer's
margin, he manufactured his own wares. He had the stove polish analyzed and launched his own line, even
managing to produce a substance that would not leave black marks on housewives' hands. He also made his
own coffee essence. At the time, coffee was considered the beverage of the rich. Meyer brewed up cheap beans
and chicory into a sort of syrup to be extended with hot water – an early form of instant coffee. Four years
after his arrival in the United States, Meyer had already made enough money to be able to marry Barbara Weil,
the daughter of Rachel Weil Meyer, with whom he had begun a love affair on the passage across. The pair set
up together in Roxborough, a suburb of Philadelphia, where they opened a shop selling stove polish and coffee essence, among other things. From 1854 to 1868, Barbara Weil and Meyer Guggenheim had 11 children.

In the meantime Meyer's head for business had lighted on new challenges. In addition to the grocery store,
he ran an import-export sideline in spices. In 1873 the spice trade was booming, and Meyer began to manufacture soap, obtaining a patent and purchasing a factory. After his competitors had sued him (unsuccess-
fully) for infringement of patent rights, Meyer sold his factory to his opponents and got out of the soap business. He turned now to the railroad and once again made a big profit in a short time before withdrawing and
starting something new: this time it was the trade in machine-made lace from Saxony and Switzerland.

The family, meanwhile, was able to afford ever grander homes in ever more desirable locations, and had even
taken to riding in a horse-drawn carriage. The four elder sons were dispatched to Europe to be educated,
particularly in lace production, while at the same time familiarizing themselves with European customs and
manners. The girls remained in the United States and were sent to the Sacred Heart convent school, where
they were readied for marriage into the better Jewish clans. When the four boys returned from their European
tour in 1877, Meyer Guggenheim founded a company, "M. Guggenheim's Sons," in which each son received an
equal share. In time, they were taken into its management.

When Meyer Guggenheim began investing in silver and lead mining in 1881, he laid the cornerstone for the
family's ascendance from ordinary riches to one of the world's greatest fortunes. Alongside its mining in-

terests, the family also began buying up and building refineries and foundries. In an elegant maneuver, the Guggenheims managed to take over their main rivals in the copper business and thus rise to become the kings of copper, the field for which they are known to this day. They used armed state troopers to break up strikes. Having started at the bottom and worked his way to the top, Meyer Guggenheim had no sympathy with his workers. If they couldn't tough it out, he reasoned, it must be their own fault.

Soon mining had become so crucial that the family divested itself of its other interests. In 1889 the Guggenheims moved to New York, which had in the meantime supplanted Philadelphia as the financial Mecca. Meyer Guggenheim died in 1905 at the age of 77, and his sons carried on the business without an interruption. By the end of the First World War the Guggenheims controlled three quarters of the world's production of copper, silver and lead along with the associated smelting works, refineries and distribution companies. By the 1920s they were among the five richest families in the U.S. The third and fourth generations were unable to further increase the family fortune, and made their name instead by giving it away. And one of them was particularly good at getting publicity for this activity.

"Mr. Kandinsky, you and I have something in common"

Solomon Guggenheim was born in 1861, the fourth of Meyer Guggenheim and Barbara Weil's children, and spent his life working for the family business. The three daughters from his marriage with Irene Rothschild were adults when he met Baroness Hilla Rebay von Ehrenwiesen in 1927. Depending on your point of view, Hilla von Rebay plays the part of either the Good Fairy or the Bad Witch in our story. The daughter of a German

general, Hilla had come to New York at the age of 36 with the intention of helping "non-objective art" achieve a breakthrough in the New World. Solomon Guggenheim, who had previously shown no interest in art, was captivated by the fascinating Baroness and began to build up what would become a world-famous art collection. He talked would-be "non-objective" artists into painting realist portraits of himself, and learned all about contemporary painting while sitting for them. Hilla taught him about the works of Vasily Kandinsky and László Moholy-Nagy, and soon Solomon had found new meaning in his life. Hilla von Rebay went on to patronize a range of artists, both famous and less well known, with Solomon's money. In 1929 Solomon traveled to Europe with his wife Irene and Hilla von Rebay, intending to meet artists and, of course, to buy art. It was on this voyage that he encountered Vasily Kandinsky, to whom he pronounced these programmatic words: "Mr. Kandinsky, you and I have something in common. You are leading a revolution in art, while my brothers and I have led a revolution in our field by financing the development of new mining techniques."

To begin with the pictures were hung in Solomon's suite at the Plaza in New York. Soon, however, he was obliged to rent rooms to contain the collection, and in 1937 he established the Solomon R. Guggenheim Foundation "for the promotion and support of art and art education." Two years later the collection moved to 24 East 54th Street, where on July 1 the Solomon R. Guggenheim Museum of Non-Objective Painting was inaugurated under the directorship of Hilla von Rebay.

It is unclear whether Hilla and Solomon had more than a platonic friendship. The fact is that their relationship lasted for the rest of their lives, even though Solomon's wife, his daughters and a whole host of art critics could not stand the Baroness, whom they accused of exploiting Guggenheim. Solomon stood by his friend when she was faced with an attack on her reputation and unjustified charges of collaboration with the Nazis. While Hilla von Rebay's impulsive, occasionally imperious nature was spellbinding for some, she also made a good many enemies. She is one of art history's most controversial figures, and has only recently received her due.

The Baroness had a vision: she wanted to champion modern art, to consecrate a temple to it. This she saw as her life's mission. Solomon Guggenheim, on the other hand, saw dealing in art as a business, too, and was not keen to make any losses. In this endeavor he was guided by Hilla, who had promised to make him and his collection world famous. In order to realize the dream of a museum specially constructed for his art collection, Guggenheim first contacted Frank Lloyd Wright as early as the 1940s. Wright was already considered the world's greatest architect, and in 1944 Guggenheim purchased a lot on 5th Avenue for which Wright designed a pilot model. But Solomon was not to see the opening of his museum. He died of cancer in 1949 at the age of 88. When his nephew Harry Guggenheim took over as President of the Foundation, his first signi-

ficant act was to fire Hilla von Rebay. But the lengthy succession process, complicated building codes and disputes between the architects and the Foundation board delayed the museum's completion for years. Finally, in spring of 1959, half a year before the museum was due to open, Frank Lloyd Wright died. When the Solomon R. Guggenheim Memorial Museum was officially inaugurated on October 21, 1959, the three main protagonists in its prehistory were absent from the ceremony. The founder and the architect were both dead, and, after years of wrangling, the Baroness, the woman who had had the original idea, was unable to find any words of praise.

Literature

Davis, John H., *Die Guggenheims: Raubritter und Menschenfreunde,* **Zurich 1978.**

Faltin, Sigrid, *Die Baroness und das Guggenheim: Hilla von Rebay – eine deutsche Künstlerin in New York,* **Bern 2005.**

Unger, Irwin and Debi Unger, *The Guggenheims: A Family History,* **New York 2005.**

Illustrations

P. 61 Group portrait: Irene Guggenheim, Vasily Kandinsky, Hilla Rebay and Solomon R. Guggenheim, 1930.

P. 62 Solomon R. Guggenheim.

P. 63 Inauguration of the Guggenheim Museum in New York, October 21, 1959.

Cheese and Bounced Checks
Niklaus Gerber (1836–1903)

At a rest stop in Monticello, Wisconsin, you will find a memorial plaque, set among stones and adorned with floral decorations. Behind it is a small pond, and a village; before it is the street that goes from New Glarus to Monroe. The plaque reads: "In 1868 Nickolaus Gerber established the first Limburger cheese factory in Green County on the Albrecht Baebler farm in Section 33, Town of New Glarus. A year later, he started the first Swiss cheese factory on the Dietrich Freitag farm in Section 1, Town of Washington ..."

The two factories were only a few miles apart. There isn't much to see there anymore. The original buildings have long since been demolished, leaving only the weathered memorials, with their scarcely legible bronze plaques from the 1930s. The plaque that now conveniently stands on the main road is meant to commemorate Gerber in our day.

Niklaus Gerber was born in 1836 in the canton of Bern. Neither the precise date (probably in October) nor his exact birthplace (possibly Steffisburg) is known. And the available sources provide no information about his family and youth. While it does seem certain that he received a training as a cheesemaker in Switzerland, it is unclear what made him leave his homeland, how he made it to the U.S., and whether (as some historians believe) he stopped off in Holland on the way. At any rate, Gerber settled in Boonville (Oneida County) in 1857. This corner of New York state was at the time a center of cheese production, and it seems likely that, in addition to practicing his trade, the professional cheesemaker learned a great deal as well, especially about sales and marketing. The claim that he was the first to produce an American Limburger, on the other hand, seems pretty far-flung, since there is no reliable evidence for it. In 1863 or 1864 Gerber moved to Illinois, founding a cheese factory in Wheeling, not far from Chicago. Success was grudging, however, and when he heard about the burgeoning dairy industry in Green County, he moved on to Wisconsin in 1868 – without his children.

Cheese or nothing

Green County south of Madison was Swiss territory. It was here that the colony of New Glarus had been founded in 1845, and along with other local farmers the immigrants from the canton of Glarus raised mostly wheat. But the land was quite hilly, and did not afford the best conditions for the crop. After some 20 years of farming the fields were exhausted, and with the fall in prices after the Civil War and an outbreak of crop disease, the happy days were truly over. Wisconsin could no longer compete with the major wheat-growing areas, now established further west.

The motto now became, "Either cheese or nothing, and happily we got cheese," as local historian Conrad Zimmerman wrote in 1884. How did this come to be? Older sources are fond of citing the Swiss affinity for cheese, which allegedly made it the most natural thing in the world for emigrants from Glarus to start producing it. This is a rather skewed way of looking at the phenomenon. While it is certainly possible that the first cheese – possibly even a Schabziger – was in fact produced by a woman from Glarus, dairy farming played a

secondary role for the first settlers, whether Swiss or not. They kept a few milk cows, and maybe even sold the butter, but cheese was made for family use only.

Cheese production only got underway when wheat farming declined and new settlers – from Ohio and New York state as well as from Europe – arrived in Green County and the rest of Wisconsin and recognized the state's potential as "America's Dairyland." This included a few Bernese, such as Rudolph Benkert (1841–1918), who is known today as the first cheesemaker in Green County. And then of course there was Niklaus Gerber.

Little is known about Gerber's private life. We don't even know exactly what he was called: he is occasionally referred to as Nikolaus, sometimes as Nicholas, often simply as Nick. The few extant photographs show a bearded man with the absent-minded gaze of a day-dreamer. These are supplemented by a few tidbits of information, for example that children loved to see him driving his horse and buggy through the region, or that he served as an umpire at a Green County Swiss-style wrestling match.

Gerber himself left no written records, and those who wrote about him did so decades after his death at a time when most of the people who knew him personally were dead. When his "true" story had long since fallen into obscurity, or had been crusted over with myths and legends. Nor does the fact that his last name was as common as dirt help researchers much.

Niklaus Gerber was married twice, the first time to Susanna, five years his senior, back in Switzerland or shortly after his arrival in the U.S. They had five children, the three sons and perhaps one of the daughters born in New York state. Their second daughter was born in Illinois in 1868, and Susanna died soon after, perhaps while still convalescing from the birth. Gerber moved on to Wisconsin, leaving his children temporarily in Illinois. Nothing more certain is known.

On October 18, 1870, he married Catharina Pfund, just 17 years old and like him from Switzerland. The couple settled in the cheese factory on Freitag farm in Washington Township. One year later Gerber sent for his children in Illinois. He had seven children in all with Catharina, four sons and three daughters. One daughter, Anna, died in childhood.

Swiss Cheese Capital of the U.S.

Niklaus Gerber started small: the Limburger factory on the Baebler farm had just 50 milk cows. And the farmers were skeptical at first, not seeing why they should take their milk to a factory. With time, however, they realized that the professional production methods not only produced better-tasting cheese, they also fetched higher prices. Gerber and his cheese factories had a prime selling point. He went on to spread his work among six to eight facilities (the precise number is not known), delegating production responsibilities and taking care of sales himself.

His name is also associated with the introduction of the cooperative farmer-factory system, whereby farmers would pool their labor, found a cheese factory, hire a cheesemaker (usually on a percentage basis) and provide their own milk as raw material. The milk would then be processed and brought to market directly or by way of a middleman. Cooperatives of this sort were common in Wisconsin.

In 1873, Green County produced a million pounds of cheddar and a million pounds of Limburger. Emmentaler, which would come to be called "Swiss cheese," was a distant third, with only around 150,000 pounds produced. In the second half of the 1880s, however, factories began to specialize in what were known as foreign cheeses: Limburger first, then Swiss cheese, which commanded higher prices on the market. In fact, so much Swiss cheese was produced that Monroe, by now the main town in Green County, could award itself the title "Swiss Cheese Capital of the U.S." It was keeping people in style: farm income was above average, with Green County always topping the ranks of prosperity among Wisconsin counties.

The cheese industry grew to dominate the local economy. In 1905, New Glarus and Washington boasted more than 22 cheese factories. There were 213 facilities in the county overall, more than in any other county in Wisconsin. Cheese accounted for almost 10% of Wisconsin's total production. Twenty years later, 4.2 million pounds of Limburger and 7.3 million pounds of Swiss cheese were produced, this last equivalent to almost a third of the total production of Swiss cheese in the U.S.

It was striking just how may Swiss immigrants with Bernese roots were part of the booming cheese industry in Green County. There were Jacob Karlen (1840–1920), Jacob Regez (1849–1914) and Gottlieb Beeler (1850–1902). But only one man had the honor of laying the cornerstone, and that man was Niklaus Gerber. This must have been what John Peter Luchsinger was thinking at any rate, when he penned his touching if rather rough and ready 1882 poem, "A Song of Cheese":

He started in and showed us how
To turn the milk to gold,
With two or three cheese factories
To which the milk was sold.

Then money soon commenced to flow,
A full, great, golden stream,
Which all into our coffers came –
It was just like a dream.

Nick Gerber was this hero's name,
Who came to us from far,
Who was our teacher in this art,
Who was our guiding star.

Cheated of his profits

Gerber was not able to make his pioneering work pay. Cheese was a pretty speculative business, and, in the words of the newspaper publisher Odell, Gerber was the "casualty of [an] early cheese battle." Production volumes had climbed so quickly in the second half of the 1870s that the relatively young markets were not able to keep pace, and prices started to sink.

This turn was to spell ruin for Gerber among others. In January of 1878 he had founded the Green County Cheese Manufacturing Company with Gottlieb Wittwer, Gottlieb Beller and Edward Ruegger. The four men joined resources, hoping to make a big splash. When it came time to sell the cheese they had amassed, however, they were unable to move it. The "cheese boom" had provoked a surplus, and prices had hit bottom.

The dramatic train of events ended in tragedy en route to Denver. Wittwer had struck out westward, hoping to find new markets for their product. Instead he met his death, probably at his own hands. In the end the three remaining partners were forced to sell their cheese for a song. Gerber seems never to have recovered from his losses in the affair.

It is not clear what happened next. Gerber moved to Brooklyn, Wisconsin, where he stayed for only a short time before heading to Monroe in 1882, where the failed entrepreneur imported cheesemaking equipment from Switzerland as a sideline to the saloon business.

But he just couldn't keep away from cheesemaking himself. In 1893 he relocated to Iowa, where he did pioneering work in the cheese industry once again, this time in Crawford County. Here too, however, he was unlucky. In his later years he is said to have tried his hand at dealing in cheese in Omaha, Nebraska, before returning to Wisconsin a broken man. Niklaus Gerber died on May 8, 1903, in Monroe.

Cheese on the head

Every Wisconsin licence plate proclaims the state "America's Dairyland." Although California long ago outstripped it as the dairy state, Wisconsin is still the number one cheese producer in the U.S. In 2004, 27% of

U.S. cheese was produced in Wisconsin, 22% in California and 8% in each of New York and Idaho. Wisconsin produces approximately 300 different types of cheese. The most popular – to judge from production volume – is mozzarella, followed by cheddar. Swiss cheese, which can be found in cheeseburgers and sandwiches, is way down on the list, making up just 1.6% of total production. At the very bottom is Limburger, once so important and now produced only in micro amounts, and only in Wisconsin.

Today's cheese industry is dominated by big companies. They produce for the mass market, for the food industry and for restaurant chains. They furnish the American consumer with the tutti-frutti range of colored cheeses to be found in the supermarkets, varieties whose yellow and orange hues are reminiscent of a Hawaiian sunset. But there are also the small manufacturers, cheesemakers who produce for the discriminating specialty foodshops, the better class of restaurants, farmers' markets and direct sales from the farm. In short, for true cheese lovers, whose numbers are growing, in Wisconsin and elsewhere.

Cheese is a central part of Wisconsin's tradition (and folklore). You can visit a wide variety of cheese factories, and Monroe is host every two years to the "Green County Cheese Days" as well as, year-round, to the Historic Cheesemaking Center. Baumgartner's Tavern, meanwhile, is famous for the best cheese sandwiches for miles around.

Wisconsinites are known to their fellow Americans as "cheeseheads," a dubious tribute to a peculiar form of local headgear. At public venues, especially sporting events, Wisconsinites are fond of wearing an artificial yellow cheese on their heads. On closer inspection, of course, it turns out that this is not just any old product: it's a piece of Swiss cheese.

Literature

Apps, Jerry, *Cheese: The Making of a Wisconsin Tradition,* Amherst, Wisconsin 1998.

Bauchle, May L., "Old Cheese Factory Records Interesting," *Hoard's Dairyman,* May 25, 1930.

Odell, Emery A., *Swiss Cheese Industry,* Monroe, Wisconsin 1936.

Illustrations

P. 66 Highway billboard advertising Wisconsin cheese, 1942.

P. 68 Postcard from Monroe, Wisconsin (c. 1910) with a portrait of Niklaus Gerber.

P. 69 Undated photograph of an old Wisconsin cheese factory with workers and deliveries by horse and carriage.

Research and Passion
Adolph F. Bandelier (1840–1914)

When Adolph François Alphonse Bandelier set out on his first research voyage in the southwestern United States in August of 1880, he was 40 years old – a late bloomer. His fame and importance as a major figure in the early history of American ethnology depend on his work in Arizona and New Mexico as well as in Mexico and South America, as does his significance for the study of native cultures, particularly those of Mexico and the southwestern United States. Ethnology, Bandelier's chosen field, was in its infancy in the late 19th and early 20th centuries, both as an academic discipline and as an area of research.

Adolph Bandelier worked as an archeologist, ethnologist, archivist, geographer, historian and natural scientist, without ever obtaining a formal education in any of these disciplines. His interdisciplinary approach allowed him to describe prehistoric native cultures in comprehensive detail, and thus to make a truly pioneering contribution to his field.

In 1916, just two years after Bandelier's death, a piece of land in New Mexico, not far from the site of the future atomic research center at Los Alamos and measuring more than 32,000 acres, was declared the Bandelier National Monument in his honor. The northern end of the Monument includes the Rito de los Frijoles Canyon, a place Bandelier called upon seeing it for the first time in October of 1880 "the grandest thing I ever saw."

Bandelier's birth in Bern on August 6, 1840, was attended by no particular omen of his successful career as a researcher and scholar. His father, Adolphe Eugène Bandelier, originally from the Bernese Jura, had studied law in Lausanne and Bern. He met his wife to be, Marie Senn Ritter, 16 years his senior, in the Swiss capital. In April of 1847 Adolphe Eugène Bandelier emigrated to Brazil, but, failing to find the new life he was looking for there, he moved on in early 1848 to the U.S. His wife and son remained behind at first in Switzerland, to follow soon after. We know nothing about the exact circumstances of Bandelier's emigration, although it seems likely that his dissatisfaction with the changed political situation in the canton of Bern (where a new constitution had been adopted) played a role.

Youth in Illinois

In October of 1848 the Bandelier family, now reunited, settled in Highland, Illinois. Barely 15 years after its establishment by the Koepflis and the Suppigers, families from Sursee in the canton of Lucerne, Highland was a lively small town with around 500 inhabitants, and growing fast. The German-speaking founders had gradually been joined by French-speaking settlers from Switzerland and France as well as by American-born Anglophones. Thirty years later Highland boasted two schools, four churches, a Catholic university, two large cereal mills, a foundry, a bank and a newspaper, as well as a population of some 1,800.

The Bandelier family settled on a farm near town. Adolphe Eugène Bandelier worked as a farmer and merchant, advised various neighbors on legal matters and served as Swiss consul for the region, which included the Mississippi Valley all the way to New Orleans and stretched eastward as far as the Appalachians. His son helped out on the farm and attended private lessons organized for him and two of the Huegy and Rhyner boys,

with whose families Adolphe had founded a bank in 1854. In February of 1855, young Adolph's mother died, a real blow to the young man.

In Highland Adolph Bandelier enjoyed a comprehensive schooling, far superior to what one might expect (to this day) from a small town in the American Midwest. His parents, his private tutor and his many contacts with educated, well-traveled friends of the family gave him a solid grounding and a healthy dose of intellectual curiosity. He spoke and wrote several languages, read a great deal and was comfortable with archeology, history, botany and zoology as well as literature and the arts.

In 1861 he married Maria Josepha (Josephine) Huegy, four years his senior. His union with Joe, as he called her, was probably the fruit of dynastic manipulations on the part of their two families, which were already united in commercial affairs. Nevertheless, the marriage seems to have been a happy one.

From business to research

In the late 1860s Bandelier embarked on a series of meteorological and climatological observations, for the Smithsonian Institution among others, while at the same time giving scholarly lectures in Highland as well as, importantly, in St. Louis, where he came into contact with the scientific community. In 1873 Bandelier made the acquaintance of the leading anthropologist and ethnographer Lewis Henry Morgan (1818–1881), with whom he was to enjoy a friendship bordering on idolatry with far-reaching consequences for his later life and, especially, his career. Indeed, one can say without exaggeration that Morgan gave Bandelier's life the decisive turn that led him finally to science. Bandelier was aware of this himself when in 1877 he wrote to Reverend M. B. Anderson, President of the University of Rochester, "I have not forgotten, nor shall I ever forget, that to your kindness I owe my connection with Mr. Morgan."

Lewis Henry Morgan's position on the cultures of the native peoples of North America was informed by a belief in the unilinear cultural and social development of human culture in general, which in practice meant that he thought all human societies could be located on a continuum from savagery to civilization. Further, given enough time and favorable conditions, every society would inevitably move up from the lowest to the highest cultural level. Morgan's position was far from being unbiased, however. According to him, by the 19th century, only the Europeans and, to a certain degree, a few Asian societies had reached the highest level of civilization. Today such a view of human civilization and its development has been replaced by a more nuanced idea of cultural plurality and equality. While Bandelier did become a champion of Morgan's unilinear evolutionism, the empiricist within him would always privately distance himself from the theory.

A cry for help from Highland

Bandelier was a busy man. By day he managed his interests at the Confidence Coal & Mining Co. and the Highland Mechanical Works, as well as, probably, working for the Rhyner Bank. His correspondence with Morgan provides some insight into his everyday life in the 1870s: "To give you an idea of what your correspondent is, allow me to say: I am at the office from 7 a.m. to 5 p.m., have to attend to a coal mine in the spare hours & only what is left of the night hours can I devote to study."

The hard work wore down Bandelier's health, not only physically but, in the end, because he was faced with a decision he would not or could not make: whether to leave the world of commerce for good and concentrate solely on scholarship. In February of 1880 he wrote to Morgan in despair: "The result of all [this mental and physical exhaustion] is that I must leave Highland for at least one or two years, taking my wife along, and settle elsewhere during that time. ... [I] ask you to assist me in finding a situation, if possible as assistant librarian or something similar to it. ... The matter is very urgent; it is one of life & death, for if I cannot find a place then I cannot leave here, & by staying here I have the perspective of becoming a helpless idiot very soon."

Morgan had anticipated this cry for help and had simultaneously written proposing a research voyage to the American southwest in the pay of the newly-founded Archaeological Institute of America (AIA). Bandelier's reaction was one of relief and enthusiasm. "Your letter has been a perfect blessing to all," he wrote on February 5, 1880; and, in the detailed diary he would from then on keep for the next 31 years, taking it with him on all of his field work, he noted, "My life's work has at last begun."

Light and shadow

The American southwest that Bandelier was to visit repeatedly for research purposes was marked not only by centuries of native settlement but also by the Spanish, present as colonists since the 16th century. Bandelier traveled miles in occasionally unbearable conditions, by foot or on horseback, alone or in company. In his neat handwriting he filled page after page of his journal, took pictures, made measurements, and drew and painted as circumstances allowed. Upon his return he began to sift through this material and to organize it, writing up reports and publishing many articles. He also found the time to write books, and not only scholarly ones: he published a novel as well. In 1881 and 1884 he did field work in Mexico, and in 1892 the Bandeliers traveled to Peru and Bolivia. Bandelier was to remain there until 1903, returning only then to the United States.

His historical and ethnological studies of American native cultures were truly groundbreaking work, both academically and practically. He was one of the first to apply the method of participant observation, before the term was even used by practitioners of the nascent discipline. By combining the methods and findings of the most disparate academic disciplines he was able to produce a dense and detailed description of the pre-historic and proto-historic native cultures he studied. This was by no means an easy undertaking, since the systematic coordination and assessment of the research findings of academic disciplines such as archeology, ethnography and history was still several years in the future.

The final days of 1892 were a time of both tragedy and new hope. The Bandeliers were in Lima when, on December 11, Joe suddenly and unexpectedly died, probably of an intestinal obstruction. She was buried the next day. Bandelier's ensuing course of action may seem bizarre, because scarcely two weeks later he was asking for the hand of Fanny Ritter, an emigrant from Zurich with whose family the Bandeliers had become friendly that past summer. Fanny, almost 30 years Bandelier's junior, accepted. Bandelier's diary entries for those last days of December are the record of his struggle with competing sentiments: his loving memory of Joe and his fear of a life without her. He was torn between feelings of loneliness and hope, and it was the latter that won out in the end. "A new life begins, a new leaf is turned over," he wrote on December 31, 1892. The couple settled in New York in 1903, where Bandelier had found work at Columbia University and the American Museum of Natural History. But his position was anything but secure. The Bandeliers were plagued by money worries and had constant recourse to private backing. Adolph's health was bad, and between 1907 and

1911 he went partially blind, recovering only slowly after an operation. At that point, however, with the generous financial support of the Carnegie Institution in Washington, he was able to carry out research in the "Archivo General" in Mexico as well as the "Archivo General de Indias" in Sevilla, this last project an old dream of his. His health deteriorated over the winter of 1913, and Adolph Bandelier died on March 18, 1914. His remains were returned to the U.S. from Seville 63 years later, cremated, and the ashes scattered above his beloved Frijoles Canyon.

Fanny remained in Seville until 1915, continuing Bandelier's archival work there. She was associated with her husband's scholarly estate until her death in 1936 in Nashville, Tennessee, but she was never able to emerge from his shadow, despite her own achievements as a researcher. Without her energetic contribution, Bandelier's final work could never have been accomplished.

Literature

Burrus, Ernest (ed.), *Adolph François Bandelier, Southwestern United States and Northwestern Mexico from the Earliest Times to 1700,* **Citta del Vaticano 1969.**

Lange, Charles H. and Caroll L. Riley, *Bandelier: The Life and Adventures of Adolph Bandelier,* **Salt Lake City 1996.**

White, Leslie A., *Pioneers in American Anthropology: The Bandelier-Morgan Letters 1873–1883,* **2 vols., Albuquerque 1940.**

Illustrations

P. 72 (l.) Adolph Bandelier with his second wife, Fanny Ritter Bandelier.

P. 72 (r.) The Bandelier family in front of their Varga Street home.

P. 75 Fieldwork team: Adolph Bandelier (next to camera), Fanny (with family dog), and four unidentified team members.

Stephan Lütolf

Tempo and Technique
Louis Chevrolet (1878–1941)

It all began with car trouble. Sometime in the spring of 1896 or 1897, so the legend goes, a breakdown occurred that led to Louis Chevrolet's emigration and subsequent success. At the time the young Chevrolet was a bicycle repairman's assistant in Beaune, in Burgundy. A wealthy American was tooling through the region in one of the very first motorcars when his vehicle broke down. Only Louis Chevrolet was able to repair the engine, and in return he received not only a tip but the American's card, with an invitation to visit the United States. The American, who is supposed to have been a descendant of the enormously wealthy railroad and shipping tycoon Cornelius Vanderbilt, told him that they could use mechanics like him there.

Jacques Chevalley, the author of a biography of Louis Chevrolet, is convinced that, of the many legends surrounding his life, this one comes the closest to the truth. Three inhabitants of Beaune confirmed that the young man repaired a tourist's motorcar, although there is no indication that this visitor came from the U.S. Chevalley believes that the Vanderbilt detail was added to the story apocryphally, after Chevrolet's emigration to the U.S. What is certain is that the young Chevrolet's first glimpse of an automobile at the end of the 19th century aroused in him a mighty passion for the new means of transportation.

From the Jura to Burgundy

Louis-Joseph Chevrolet was born on December 25, 1878, in La Chaux-de-Fonds, the second son of a poor watchmaker, Joseph Félicien Chevrolet. Like his father, his mother, Marie-Anne Angéline, née Mahon, came from what is now the Swiss canton of Jura, where the young Louis Chevrolet spent the first years of his life, in the villages of Bonfol and Beurnevésin. As the family grew to include five children, its poverty was not alleviated, and a crisis in the watchmaking industry was probably behind the family's emigration to France in April 1887. It remains unclear why they should have sought a better life in the little town of Beaune in Burgundy. Joseph Félicien opened a watchmaker's business there, but his family, which now counted nine members, continued to live an impoverished existence in France. The children were taken out of school at the tender age of eleven and made to contribute to the family's livelihood. From about 1889 on, Louis was employed at the Roblin mechanical workshop in Beaune. His very first job awoke in him an enthusiasm for motors.

According to C.W. Van Ranst, a colleague and friend of the automotive pioneer's, Chevrolet first held a motor in his hands around 1893 when, just 14 years old, he got his boss's motorized tricycle running again. Roblin also sold bicycles, and it was thus that Chevrolet developed a passion for racing, competing successfully in regional events from 1895 on. More than a dozen wins brought him glory, as well as funds.

Chevrolet left Beaune in 1899 for the outskirts of Paris and work in a new automotive plant. The 20-year-old had lost his taste for Europe, however, and was saving money for the trip to North America. What motivated his emigration is the stuff of speculation. Chevrolet probably assumed that the future of the automobile was in the U.S., and he was also in contact with two friends who had emigrated to the U.S. earlier. Accompanied by a colleague, Chevrolet arrived in Montreal in 1900. The two emigrants were doubtless led by linguistic

considerations to begin their adventure in Canada. They found work in Montreal as drivers and mechanics, but Chevrolet soon saw that his chances were better south of the border. In April 1901 he arrived in New York, where he found a position in a Brooklyn garage run by William Walter, originally of Biel in Switzerland.

The "dare devil Frenchman"

Chevrolet made his name as a mechanic and in 1901 went to work for the famous French automobile manufacturer De Dion-Bouton, switching the next year to Fiat. Chevrolet's father died in France in 1902, and his mother and the three youngest siblings, Arthur, Marthe and Gaston, followed Louis to the U.S. His elder sisters, Fanny and Berthe, had already taken up their brother's invitation a year earlier and had found work in New York as seamstresses. Only Alfred, the eldest of the seven siblings, now remained in France.

Chevrolet's breakthrough came in 1905. The young mechanic had become known as a talented driver, and he made his big appearance in May 20 of that year in a remodeled hippodrome in New York. He won his very first car race, setting a new world record with a Fiat automobile. Chevrolet covered a mile in 52.8 seconds, at an average velocity of 68.2 mph. The victor was awarded, among other things, a watch engraved with the name of the sponsor, Walter Percy Chrysler.

That same year Chevrolet broke his own record for the mile as well as setting a new record for the 68-mile race. It had taken the emigrant just a few years to become an American celebrity. Journalists called Chevrolet the "dare devil Frenchman" because of his driving style and his look, which included a "Gallic" moustache, a

cigarette dangling carelessly from the corner of his mouth and a sullen expression, and soon became the trademark of the nationally known race driver. Between his first two racing victories, in July 1905, Chevrolet married Suzanne Treyvoux. The young Frenchwoman, who had only recently arrived in New York with her parents from Paris, would bear him two children, Charles and Alfred.

Chevrolet fully lived up to his reputation as a "dare devil Frenchman." If he didn't come in first, it was usually because he had been involved in a wreck. Legend has it that, of the 15 years he took part in races, he spent three in hospital recovering from injuries. It is true that Chevrolet narrowly escaped death on the race track countless times, and four of the mechanics who rode with him perished. But it wasn't all just luck: Chevrolet's skill saved him from dying on the course. In 1919 his car suddenly caught fire during a race while he was doing 115 mph. If he had braked at that speed, Chevrolet's vehicle would probably have turned over, so he stood straight up in his seat, piloted the burning car off the course and crashed it into a wall. Driver and mechanic alike got away with burns.

When his younger brother Gaston died, Chevrolet was at last moved to abandon his career in racing. Gaston, America's most successful race-car driver in 1920, died in an accident in November of that year during a race in Beverly Hills. Chevrolet raced only once more after that day, winning a boating event in Florida in 1925. Chevrolet's competitive spirit remained alive even after his retirement from race-car driving, however, and he went on to triumph at golf and marksmanship.

The luckless builder

Chevrolet was not only a celebrated race-car driver, he was also a great pioneer in the automotive world. The burgeoning car industry sat up and took notice of his successes on the race course, realizing that the many spectators made racing events into great advertising opportunities. William Crapo Durant, a clever business-man who had sold everything from cigarettes to groceries and real estate, took over the Buick car company in 1904. In 1907 Durant signed Chevrolet on as a race-car driver and Buick builder, while Louis's brother Arthur became the businessman's private chauffeur. One year later Durant took over Cadillac and Oldsmobile to form the General Motors Company, only to leave the company in 1910 over a dispute.

Now Durant was planning to get back into the automobile business – with Chevrolet. The entrepreneur aimed to use the famous name to rival General Motors, and in late 1911 he founded the Chevrolet Motor Car Compa-ny in Detroit. Chevrolet himself held only a few shares in the company that bore his name, but he did receive a handsome salary and had a free hand with building. Chevrolet developed the Classic Six, an elegant luxury car with six cylinders. The series went into production in 1912, but its steep price of $2,150 placed it out of competition with the much cheaper Ford T. This, of course, foiled Durant's plans, and he drove Chevrolet to develop smaller, more affordable models. For his part, Chevrolet's passion for racing and mechanics forbade him to do anything but dream up big beautiful cars, and when Durant took advantage of Chevrolet's absence in Europe to reorganize the factory, the two men fell out. Chevrolet left the company at the end of 1913, thus losing the rights to his own name. The Classic Six was to remain the only vehicle Chevrolet built under that

name. Durant went on to turn out cheap cars, and enjoyed great success in 1914. In 1917 he used a share swap to take back control of General Motors, and integrated the Chevrolet brand into the company in 1918. By 1927 Chevrolet was overtaking Ford in production. The design of the Chevrolet logo, which has remained unchanged to this day, is said to have been discovered by Durant in the pattern of a carpet in a Paris hotel. Meanwhile, true to his motto "Never give up," which decorates his bust in the memorial erected at the Indianapolis Speedway, Chevrolet continued with his own work. He was obsessed with the idea of building a light-weight car, and was among the first to deploy aluminum alloys. His small-car project foundered when he couldn't scare up enough investors, but Chevrolet was successful with his Frontenac race car, later also known as the Monroe. In 1921 he and his brothers opened a plant in Indianapolis and worked for Ford, among others. An economic crisis forced them into bankruptcy in 1923, but Chevrolet went on building and in 1926 founded an airplane motor factory with his brother Arthur. The two argued soon after, however, and the crash of 1929 carried off both this latest project and Chevrolet's assets. He took his family back to Detroit in 1933, where he worked as an ordinary mechanic at the company with his name. By this point eight million Chevrolets had been produced and, while the brand was world-renowned, its namesake was unknown and forgotten. While there is no record of Chevrolet's feelings about the fact that millions of cars bore his name while he had been unable to profit from it, he is said to have repeatedly stressed his failure as a builder.

Chevrolet was not able to escape further setbacks. In 1934 he suffered a severe stroke, from which he never fully recovered. That same year his son Charles died of an illness at the age of 27, and Chevrolet's sister's

Picture Section.
Rotogravure, in
Two Parts: **Part 5**
The New York Times
Sunday,
September 30, 1917.

CAPT. GEORGES GUYNEMER.
Most Famous of French Aviators, With an Official Credit of Fifty Aerial Victories, and Now Reported Dead, Conversing with General Franchet D'Esperey Early in September When He Received the Last Decoration Bestowed Upon Him. He Had Received Practically Every Decoration His Country Could Give, a Few of Which He is Here Wearing.
(Pictorial Press.)

NAVAL OBSERVATION BALLOON AND SEAPLANE, AMERICAN "SENTINELS OF THE SKY," FLYING HIGH ABOVE A CRUISER TO WHICH THEY ARE ATTACHED.
From a New Photograph, Other Details Regarding Which Are Withheld at the Request of the Navy Censor.

REMARKABLE PHOTOGRAPH OF "SENTINELS OF THE SKY" HOVERING OVER THE PASUBIO, ONE OF THE HIGHEST INACCESSIBLE PEAKS OF THE ALPS, NEAR THE BOUNDARY LINE BETWEEN AUSTRIA AND ITALY. On the Left Is the Austrian "Aviatik," and, on the Right, the Italian "Nieuport" Machine, Flying in Opposite Directions, Both Apparently Manoeuvring for Positions from Which to Attack.

Louis Chevrolet Crossing the Line, Winner of the $10,000 Gold Trophy Donated by Harry S. Harkness, Having Covered the 100-Mile Course Over the Sheepshead Bay Speedway at an Average of 111 Miles an Hour, a New World's Record.
(Times Photo Service.)

VISCOUNT READING, Lord Chief Justice of England, and Colonel E. D. Swinton, Called the "Father" and Promoter of the British "Tank." Lord Reading and Colonel Swinton Are Here on a Special Financial Mission for the British Government.
(C Int. Film Service.)

YOUNG LIONESS CUB, ADOPTED AS A REGIMENTAL MASCOT BY ONE OF THE UNITS WITH GENERAL PERSHING ON THE FRENCH FRONT, IN THE ARMS OF HER SPECIAL CUSTODIAN.

LOUIS CHEVROLET RECEIVING THE HARKNESS $10,000 TROPHY, AND BESIDE HIM HIS MECHANICIAN, RAY RIGGY, WITH HIS OWN TRIBUTE OF AMERICAN BEAUTIES.
(C A. P. A.)

"SPEED DEMONS" TAKING THE SOUTH END TURN OF THE SHEEPSHEAD BAY

POWERFUL ITALIAN GUN, EMPLOYED ON THE ISONZO FRONT, IS HERE SHOWN MOUNTED PARTLY ON AN AUTOMOBILE TRUCK AND PARTLY ON ENDLESS CATERPILLAR CHAINS, SUCH AS ARE USED FOR THE BRITISH "TANKS," TO FACILITATE MOUNTAIN CLIMBING.
(C Kadel & Herbert.)

SPEEDWAY IN THE HARKNESS GOLD TROPHY RACE.
(Paul Thompson.)

house in New Jersey was destroyed by fire. This put an end to his hopes of success as a builder, for Chevrolet had stored all of his plans and drawings there. Chevrolet died in his house near Detroit on June 6, 1941, at the age of 63. Hardly anyone paid notice to the death of the once famous race-car driver and brilliant builder as the Second World War raged on. It was not until 1975 that the Chevrolet Memorial was unveiled in Indianapolis, and in 1991 Bonfol was graced with the Place Louis Chevrolet. Chevrolet did not maintain a strong connection to Switzerland during his life in America. The automotive pioneer, who became an American citizen in 1915, never returned to the country of his birth after leaving it for the U.S. Only his thick French accent, which he kept until his death, served as a reminder of his origins.

Literature

Barras, Pierre, *L'aventure Louis Chevrolet,* Porrentruy 1991.

Chevalley, Jacques, *Chevrolet: Un nom de famille,* Beaune 1992.

Schmid, Hans Rudolf, "Louis Chevrolet (1878–1941): Pionier des Automobils in den Vereinigten Staaten, Begründer einer Weltmarke,"
Verein für wirtschaftshistorische Studien (ed.), *Schweizer Pioniere der Wirtschaft und Technik,* Zurich 1960, pp. 47–67.

Illustrations

P. 78 Chevrolet in the Darracq V8 in which he set a world record in 1906.

P. 79 Chevrolet and Amelia Earhart, race car driver and in 1932 the first woman to fly solo across the Atlantic.

P. 80 Chevrolet factory in Baltimore, 1935.

P. 81 Group portrait in front of the Motor Car Company, 1911. Chevrolet in white coat with the first Chevrolet Classic Six.

P. 82 Picture section of the *New York Times,* September 30, 1917.

P. 83 Louis Chevrolet as American icon.

Bridges and Visions
Othmar H. Ammann (1879–1965)

Othmar Hermann Ammann will go down in New York history as "the" bridge builder. In 1964, not long before his death, he was awarded the National Medal of Science by President Lyndon B. Johnson, the first time such a distinction was granted to a civil engineer. It was in a sense his crowning achievement. And yet the Swiss-born Ammann had long since set himself his own monument, in the form of his great bridges.

Ammann was born on March 26, 1879, in Feuerthalen, near Schaffhausen in the canton of Zurich. It was here that he spent the first years of his life, until his father's manufacture, and the family home, were moved to Bendlikon, near Kilchberg further south in the canton, in 1887. After graduating from industrial college in Zurich he went on to the Swiss Federal Institute of Technology (ETH) in that city, where he majored in civil engineering. In 1902, with a first-rate degree in hand, Ammann took up his first position at Wartmann & Valette, a Swiss steel construction firm, and was sent to Geneva to plan the Mont-Blanc bridge. Not long after, however, he went to work for Buchheim and Heistler, a construction firm in Frankfurt am Main in Germany, where the ambitious young engineer was able to profit from practical experience working with reinforced concrete. But he did not stay for long. Professor Karl E. Hilgard of the ETH, long-time bridge engineer for the Northern Pacific Railroad, told his former student about the United States – and Ammann, mindful of his career, promptly emigrated in 1904.

One year later, back in Switzerland on vacation, Ammann married his childhood sweetheart Lilly Wehrli, with whom he would go on to have three children. Werner was born in 1906, Georg Andrew in 1910 and Margot in 1922. In 1935, after the death of his first wife two years earlier, Ammann married Kläry Nötzli, the widow of another immigrant civil engineer.

Great projects

American cities were changing rapidly. Skyscrapers were going up in Chicago, in New York construction had begun on a subway (1904), and in San Francisco an earthquake and fire had destroyed whole sections of town. This was the world in which Othmar Ammann found himself, freshly arrived at the age of 25. It didn't take him long to get work at Joseph Mayer's engineering firm on Broadway in New York, where he learned for the first time about the plan to connect Manhattan with residential New Jersey by means of a bridge across the one-mile broad Hudson. Life in Greater New York had been utterly transformed by the advent of motorized transport at the end of the 19th century, and just short of 20 ferry connections across the Hudson were having a harder time every year handling the increasing traffic. In memoirs composed in 1955, Ammann writes that his interest in building a bridge across the Hudson had been aroused shortly after his arrival in New York, when he had the idea for a daring feat of engineering while out for a stroll along the Palisades Cliffs. His dream was of a construction 3,000 feet across, nearly twice the span of the longest bridge standing at the time. Once gripped by this vision, he could not rest, and he became an avid follower of contemporary bridge-building.

When the gigantic St. Lawrence River Bridge near Quebec collapsed on August 19, 1907, Ammann came one step closer to making his dream a reality. His boss at the Pennsylvania Steel Co., where he had been employed since 1905, recommended the 28-year-old Swiss to the engineer charged with investigating the collapse, and the two soon discovered that several braces had been omitted from the construction in order to save money. Ammann went on to work on the new St. Lawrence River Bridge at the offices of Kunz & Schneider, until in 1912 he received a position with Gustav Lindenthal (1850–1926) of New York, at the time the leading bridge engineer in the U.S. Lindenthal, himself an immigrant to the country, had done his training as an engineer in Dresden, and left Germany in 1874. He had been commissioned by the Atlantic-Great Western Railroad to build the Hell Gate Bridge, a four-track railway connection across the East River in New York. At the time the world's longest steel arch bridge with a span of 977 feet, the Hell Gate Bridge gave the young assistant engineer plenty of trouble, until he was interrupted in his work by the outbreak of the First World War. In August 1914 there were rumors that the Germans had invaded Switzerland, and Ammann immediately decided to return and enlist as a lieutenant for what he imagined was the defense of his homeland. Just four months later, however, Ammann was back at work in Lindenthal's office, where the Hell Gate Bridge had not yet been completed.

Professional breakthrough

Once this bridge and the Sciotoville Railroad Bridge over the Ohio River had been completed in 1917, Lindenthal was forced by the recession and the fact that the U.S. had declared war on Germany to let Ammann go. Ammann considered joining the American army until his former employer offered him a position as manager of a brickworks in New Jersey, where he was able to demonstrate his organizational talent before returning to Lindenthal's office at the end of the decade. His boss was once again hard at work on bridge projects across the Hudson.

There was no question that New York needed a connection to New Jersey; the only point of contention was where to build the bridge. Lindenthal and Ammann had both come to the U.S. looking for a professional challenge, and they were both admirers of construction in the grand style. But they had their differences, too, for instance when it came to their grasp of politics. While Lindenthal favored a gigantic two-storey bridge with 20 lanes and 12 railway tracks at the level of 57th Street, a project that would have cost more than $200,000,000 for the structure alone, Ammann recognized that such a plan was hopeless. He could see that neither the political will nor the necessary financing was available, and the pragmatist in him wondered how Manhattan could deal with the increased volume of traffic. His answer: a suspension bridge connecting 179th Street to the Palisades Cliffs, 3,500 feet long with initially only an upper level with eight lanes, to which a lower level, with four railway tracks or six lanes, could later be added. The two men soon fell out, with Lindenthal calling Ammann shortsighted in the face of his own millennial visions. Ammann left Lindenthal in 1923 to come to terms with the political and technical challenges on his own. He found support among Swiss associates, the owners of Schwarzenbach, Huber + Co., silk manufacturers in New York, who granted him office space. In addition to his daily drafting work, the normally reserved Ammann, an American citizen since 1924, now spent evenings lobbying for his bridge project among the members of various committees, political and otherwise. In early 1925, with the legal basis established in New York and New Jersey as well as by the Congress in

Washington, the long-awaited decision was made, and on July 1, 1925, Ammann was appointed Chief Engineer of the Port Authority of New York, with responsibility not only for the port itself but also for connections between the two neighboring states. Under Ammann, work proceeded simultaneously on four bridge projects: the Goethals Bridge and Outerbridge Crossing, the first fixed links between Staten Island and New Jersey; the Hudson River Bridge, today known as the George Washington Bridge; and the Bayonne Bridge. Ammann had made it as the 20th century's leading bridge-builder.

The George Washington Bridge was the first ever to span a distance of 3,500 feet, while the Bayonne Bridge was the largest arch bridge ever built. The two structures were inaugurated within weeks of each other, on October 24 and November 15, 1931. Franklin D. Roosevelt, then Governor of New York, praised the Swiss engineer on both occasions. As bridge-builder and chief engineer of New York's Port Authority, Roosevelt said, Ammann was responsible not only for the bridges' design but also for their fast and successful completion. His work, noted Roosevelt, "marks a new high standard in public service."

In 1934, the city's own organization, the Triborough Bridge Authority, was also able to secure Ammann's services, and he was charged with the building of the Triborough Bridge, which opened on July 11, 1936. It was also during this period that San Francisco's Golden Gate Bridge was built, on whose planning Ammann evidently worked closely, according to an interview. The city's chief engineer had asked him for help as early as 1917, and two years later Ammann traveled to the West Coast with a first design. Popular resistance, however, stalled construction, and it was not until 1937 that the Golden Gate Bridge was opened to traffic.

Ammann did not rest in the wake of these enormous projects. He went on to complete the second tunnel under the Hudson, the 1½-mile long Lincoln Tunnel, inaugurated in December 1937; he designed Battery Brooklyn Bridge to connect the southern end of Manhattan to Brooklyn, a plan that was defeated by resistance from Brooklyn; and he built the extremely elegant Bronx-Whitestone Bridge over the East River, a suspension bridge with a main span of 2,300 feet.

Tireless productivity

In 1939, at the age of 60, Ammann withdrew from both of his public functions, with the Port Authority and the Triborough Bridge Authority. He intended to take on only consulting roles in major bridge projects in future, and one year later he had one: the collapse of the Tacoma Narrows Bridge in 1940 saw the relevant authorities commissioning Ammann and two other experts to carry out an investigation. Ammann developed a stiffness index, which he then calculated for more than 30 bridges.

Further projects followed, and Ammann never really retired. Together with a landscape architect he formulated designs for modern parkways with appropriate overpasses, and in 1946 he joined forces with a well-known American concrete engineer to found Ammann & Whitney, still functioning to this day. Among the projects completed by the firm are the Walt Whitman Bridge near Philadelphia, built in 1957, the Throgs Neck Bridge near New York, built in 1961 in preparation for the World's Fair, and the lower deck of the George Washington Bridge, added in 1962 and featuring six more lanes. A symbol of America's unlimited mobility, the George Washington Bridge, with a total of 14 lanes, boasted the greatest traffic capacity, and was used in 1977 by some 78,000,000 vehicles, or around ten vehicles per minute and lane.

But the jewel in Ammann's crown is the Verrazano Narrows Bridge, opened on November 21, 1964. With its 12 lanes on two levels, it was able to break a series of records. Although its main span (4,260 feet) is only 60 feet longer than that of the Golden Gate Bridge, the Verrazano is 75% heavier than its Californian rival. Ammann called the planning and construction of the Verrazano Narrows Bridge a major challenge to the engineering profession. Its completion was a testament to successful cooperation among private and public organizations, as well as to the great progress made by science and technology, without which it would never have been erected.

The renowned bridge-builder died in 1965 at the advanced age of 86. The great bridges in and around New York are his monument. For his part, he had this to say about his life's work: "The road to success is open to anyone who is not put off by hard work and the need for daring and endurance."

Literature

Billington, David P., *The Art of Structural Design: A Swiss Legacy,* Princeton 2003.

Doig, Jameson W., "Politics and the Engineering Mind: O. H. Ammann and the Hidden Story of the George Washington Bridge," in *Yearbook of German-American Studies* 25 (1990), pp. 151–199.

Stüssi, Fritz, *Othmar H. Ammann – sein Beitrag zur Entwicklung des Brückenbaus,* Schriftenreihe des Instituts für Geschichte und Theorie der Architektur an der ETH, vol. 7, Basel 1974.

Widmer, Urs, "Othmar Hermann Ammann, 1879–1965: His Way to Great Bridges," in *Swiss American Historical Society Newsletter* 15 (1979), pp. 5–6.

Illustrations

P. 84 Othmar H. Ammann with the George Washington Bridge. With this bridge Ammann was the first to span a distance of 3,500 feet in the 1930s.

P. 87 Verrazano Narrows Bridge, built 1959-1964.

P. 88 (above) Golden Gate Bridge, San Francisco.

P. 88 (below) Bronx Whitestone Bridge, New York.

P. 89 Othmar H. Ammann with the Verrazano Narrows Bridge (undated photograph).

Hard-Headedness and Hawaiian Guitars
Adolph Rickenbacher (1887–1976)

He was a character, they say. "Mister Adolph gave everyone a calling card printed with the words 'Adolph Rickenbacher, Father of the Electric Guitar'," recalls Margarita, veteran member of the cleaning staff at the Atria Acacia Senior Living Group, a pretty colonnaded building at the corner of Acacia and Chapman in Fullerton, California. Early on March 7, 1976, Rickenbacher, who had been suffering from cancer, succumbed to acute circulatory failure at the Gordon Lane Convalescent Hospital. Rickenbacher was the embodiment of the American dream, the one that still had a chance of coming true for immigrants arriving between 1890 and 1924. He had come in 1891 as a poor kid, and he died a wealthy man.

As the "father of the electric guitar," however, he has achieved immortality. Far from being "Born in the USA," the prototypical rock 'n' roll instrument would have been unthinkable without the work of a Swiss immigrant. And, while his partner George Beauchamp may have been indispensable to the invention of the pick-up, which turns the oscillations of the steel strings into electrical energy, the company that first patented and manufactured the electric guitar bears Rickenbacher's name, ever so slightly Americanized as Rickenbacker.

Superstars like the Beatles, the Who, the Byrds, Motörhead, Creedence Clearwater Revival, Tom Petty, U2's The Edge, the Smiths, Radiohead, country rebel Dwight Yoakam and Peter Buck of R.E.M. have made the "Rick" a legend. The electric guitar is probably the biggest icon in U.S. pop culture, and generations of people to this day still associate a whole attitude to life with the instrument, with the poses they struck, the fantasies they had, and the youthful rebellions it stirred up. Currently guitar rock is enjoying a renaissance, after an interregnum in the 1990s featuring the guitar-free sounds of rap and house music. And what is the instrument of choice for top bands on both sides of the pond, whether Franz Ferdinand of Scotland or the Strokes of New York? The Rickenbacker.

A family of have-nots

It was a home birth. Adolf Adam Riggenbacher – as his last name was originally spelled – first saw the light of day on April 1, 1887, born into a poor family living at number 7 Gemsberg Street in the middle of Basel. His parents rented their apartment in the half-timbered house, built in 1291, from a bookbinder. Adolf senior ran a small cabinetmaker's business; his wife Elisabeth, née Wyss, had brought a child from a previous marriage into the family, Adolf junior's half-brother Oscar. While the economic gloom of the 1870s had lifted, the rich had fled the inner city for the suburbs, leaving the narrow, crowded old town to the have-nots.

On October 1, 1891, the family left Basel for a better life in the New World, drawn by letters from the many relatives already living in the U.S. (the family's ancestors had been emigrating since 1734). The Rickenbachers sailed out of Le Havre on the *La Bretagne* and arrived in Castle Garden, New York, on October 12, 1891: Adolf senior, Elisabeth, entered in the passenger list as "Louise," and the children Oscar (11), Emma (seven), Adolf junior (age four, although registered by the authorities as a two-year-old), and the new-born, Robert. One daughter had died before the departure, from burns sustained when she fell into an open campfire.

Those who made the week-long crossing recalled it later as a time of deprivation, with a brutal crew. "The livestock on the ship was treated better than the people," one of Rickenbacher's nieces reported. When the ship docked at the south end of Manhattan, its passengers were met by a dispiriting sight. Unseasonably cold weather (40 degrees) had practically obscured the Statue of Liberty, which had been standing on Bedloe's Island for just five years at that point. The new arrivals received tomatoes to eat, which Adolf senior warned those near him not to eat, saying they were poisonous, "forbidden love apples." It was all a ruse, of course: he collected the discarded tomatoes and was thus able to see his family through the days of customs formalities and medical checks.

In 1893 the family reached Columbus, Ohio, a short-lived paradise. Elisabeth died shortly after their arrival; Adolf senior lost both his legs in a train accident and began to drink to ease the pain and grief. Soon he could no longer care for his children, who roamed about, hungry and neglected. Emma rescued her younger brothers from an icy death when she found them, covered with snow, asleep in a doorway. With her rudimentary English she found work as a maid with a wealthy family in the southern end of town, with permission to lodge Adolf junior and Robert in her room as well. For seven years Emma raised them there.

With a mixture of skill and luck, young Adolf Rickenbacher was able to escape his family's fate. A frail man with sloping shoulders and ears that stuck out, he made up in brains what he lacked in looks. The vertical furrow in his forehead gave his young features a serious cast, although there was a twinkle in the eyes that peered out from under heavy eyebrows. He was a charmer. While still in Ohio, Adolph (as he was now writing his name) fell in love with Charlotte ("Lottie") Kammerer, the daughter of German immigrants to Pennsylvania who had grown rich in the oil business. Lottie herself worked in Columbus for the family firm as a secretary. Later on, Rickenbacher's financial fortunes were said to have changed with the marriage. The couple lived in Illinois until 1918, when they moved to California. Their earliest recorded abode there was at 4910 Angeles Vista Boulevard in Los Angeles, not a particularly fashionable address.

But the "Father of the Electric Guitar" was to end up living high on the hog. In the 1950s he had a house built on a prestigious hill-side site in Fullerton, high above Los Angeles, paying what was then the hair-raising sum of $200,000 for the spread at 1801 Vista Lomitas Drive, complete with guesthouse and swimming pool. Rickenbacher designed the place himself, mod cons and all. He dreamed up a ventilation system that purified the air, and later boasted that he hadn't dusted in 20 years. Seated on his own tractor he planted an orange grove, and on fine days he could see the ocean from there. Because his Lottie was crazy about one-armed bandits, he used to drive her once a month in his 1965 Ford LTD to play the casinos in Las Vegas. The childless couple could afford such luxuries.

Adolph must have spoken Basel dialect as a boy, "but in the end his accent was California through and through," reports his last neighbor, Bob Genc, a senior with a tan and a cowboy hat who continues to practice as a dentist long past retirement age. Everyone who knew him says that Rickenbacher was "a character," including Genc. "Oh, *Ay-dolph* was a real cut-up! You would go to visit him and he'd show you a picture of couples dancing and all the guys had erections," says Genc, shaking his head with amusement. "In the end, after his wife's death, we used to take him to a restaurant with a view of the airport. He used to watch the planes taking off and landing. It reminded him of Eddie."

Eddie Rickenbacker, Adolph's famous second cousin, shot down 26 German fighter planes in the First World War. He was known as the "Ace of Aces" and was awarded the Congressional Medal of Honor. It was said that Adolph, ever the canny businessman, changed his name to Rickenbacker in the late 1930s in order to profit from his cousin's renown. Others believe that the original spelling was simply "too German" for him, an impression he was eager to avoid as the Second World War drew ever closer. Nevertheless, the name change was purely for the office: he still spelled his name with a "ch" in personal correspondence. Rickenbacher evidently remained closely connected to Switzerland until his death. There is proof of this in the last remaining token of his residence on Vista Lomitas Drive: when his home was torn down in 2002 to make way for three new houses, the wrecking crew left a ten-foot tall, cast-iron sign, half covered by underbrush and palm leaves, emblazoned with the name "Rickenbacher."

Iron, die-casting, metal parts: that was his trade. He must have been reminded of his father's workshop in Basel when in 1920 he set up the Rickenbacher Manufacturing Company at 6105 South Western Avenue in Los Angeles. Soon he was turning out compression moulds, tools and screw threads, casting metal parts and punching out plastic components – and making a great success of it. His first major client was the National guitar factory, for which he produced housings and aluminum parts for use in its legendary "National Steel Guitars," metal instruments with built-in aluminum resonators.

The invention of the "frying pan"

The Texan guitarist George Beauchamp, the originator of the National's design, was frustrated by the failure of his instrument to make itself heard over the combined sound of a whole orchestra and got to work on a louder guitar. Together with Paul Barth, Beauchamp created what he called a "pick-up" out of copper wire and a couple of horseshoe magnets, an electromagnetic transmitter that paved the way for the electric guitar. In 1931, with Rickenbacher in his studio, the three men assembled the wooden prototype of an electric Hawaiian guitar to be held in the lap. This primitive electric guitar was dubbed the "frying pan" because of its awkward shape. The original today hangs in the office of the current owner of the Rickenbacker International Corporation in Santa Ana, John Hall. "It was Beauchamp's idea, and Rickenbacher carried it out – as well as financing it," says Hall, 56.

And Rickenbacher would need to be a very patient patron. Barth, Beauchamp and he founded the Ro-Pat-In company and began readying their "frying pan," now with an aluminum housing, for mass production. But musicians were skeptical. "All the bands were afraid to use it," recalls Rickenbacher, "because they thought a tube might blow in the middle of a show." And wouldn't you know it, during a live stage show a technical glitch had the radio station KHJ Los Angeles suddenly being broadcast through the speakers instead of guitar sound. Rickenbacher and Beauchamp were howled out of the theater. In 1932 Ro-Pat-In sold a mere dozen guitars, with Rickenbacher's tool factory underwriting the losses. "After about two years of hard work and spending about hundred-fifty thousand dollars we were ready to give up," Rickenbacher was later to recall.

But then, out of the blue, a Hawaiian orchestra ordered a complete line of electrical instruments, steel and Spanish guitars, mandolin and bass. Rickenbacher and his people worked around the clock for two months to get the instruments ready – only to have the whole shipment stolen the night before delivery. Rickenbacher figured it was an inside job. Work began from square one, and this time the pieces were delivered. But they

were never paid for. Was this the end? Just about. Thanks to a guitarist with a job at a radio station, however, they were able to make a breakthrough. The musician used the airwaves to stir up his colleagues' enthusiasm for the new invention, and when an order for 500 instruments came in from Chicago, the "Rick" was on its way. Soon Rickenbacher was supplying the world with instruments.

In 1934 the company's name was changed to the Electro String Instrument Corporation, and from then on every instrument bore the inscription "Rickenbacher Electro". A patent was applied for in 1932, but it took years to be approved. Rickenbacher and Beauchamp finally sent a music group to Washington to play for the severe patent officers, convincing them at last that the electric guitar actually worked. By the time the patent was issued on August 10, 1937, other brands had long since come on the market.

In 1935 Rickenbacher manufactured the first guitar body out of the artificial substance Bakelite, thus giving birth to the so-called "solid-body" guitar without a resonance chamber. Business was booming, and in 1940 Beauchamp sold his share to Rickenbacher. The company now belonged to Adolph and Charlotte alone. Despite the depression of the 1930s, Rickenbacher was now living in style in Beverly Hills, a made man with a fleet of seven automobiles. Was he just a blowhard? After all, he hadn't invented the electric guitar anymore than Elvis had invented rock 'n' roll: a whole slew of anonymous predecessors had done that. People had been experimenting with Rickenbacher's "invention" since the 19th century. Rickenbacher (like Elvis) was simply in the right place at the right time, able to capitalize on his hard-headedness and financial comfort to hit pay dirt with a mass phenomenon. "Inventor of the Electric Guitar" would have been a bit pretentious – "Father" is about right.

"Rickenbacker" lives on

At the company's current headquarters on South Main Street in Santa Ana, from the street a nondescript green factory shed, 65 employees are doing precision handwork, among them many Latinos and Vietnamese. They are using a machine calibrated to a thousandth of a millimeter to cut guitar bodies out of maple wood, spraying on paint, drilling, soldering, gluing, winding copper wire and attaching magnetic plates to the pick-ups. "The competition has its pick-ups made in Korea, China and Mexico," says John Hall. "But we invented ours, so we're still making them ourselves 75 years later." His father, F. C. Hall, bought the company from Rickenbacher, then 66 years old, on December 17, 1953, a few weeks before Bill Haley and Elvis Presley exploded on the scene and rock 'n' roll was born. Rickenbacher went on to build his villa in Fullerton and purchase a ranch in Redlands, California.

"It is a tribute to the technology of 1931 that it is pretty much unchanged to this day," says Hall. Of all the famous brands of guitar known the world over, the Rickenbacker has a reputation as a little bijou, the only one "proudly produced in the USA" while the competition has been manufacturing parts or even entire instruments on the cheap in the Far East for some time now. "We are the Porsche of guitars: high quality, low production," says Hall, "each one is a piece of artistic craftsmanship." The CEO has only one regret: his desire to have the Swiss cross engraved onto the some 10,000 instruments his crew produces annually was foiled by the Swiss government.

Richard Burke, Rickenbacher's former production manager, recalls that his ex-boss continued to check that everything was going well even after he had ceased to own the company. "He would come by the factory almost every week, always ready for a joke, and always in the mood for a deal. One week before he died he was still trying to sell me a Buick." Only 25 people attended his funeral. "It was a shame! Adolph deserved better. But the Rickenbacker guitar! He would have been very happy to know that it still bears his name." Adolph Rickenbacher was "a character" even if he did occasionally also indulge in morbid humor. Orphaned young, he had been forced to make it all alone in a foreign country. And, although his success was due to his many talents, there was one thing the Father of the Electric Guitar never did manage to learn how to do: play the guitar.

Literature
Bacon, Tony and Paul Day, *The Rickenbacker Book: A Complete History of Rickenbacker Electric Guitars,* San Francisco 1994.
Rickenbacker, Capt. Eddie V., *Fighting the Flying Circus,* Garden City 1965.

Illustrations
P.93 Jimi Hendrix in concert on the Isle of Wight, England, 1970.
P.95 John Lennon during a performance at Madison Square Garden in New York, on August 31, 1972.
P.96 Melissa Etheridge at the Rock for Choice Concert in the Hollywood Palladium, January 23, 2004.
P.97 Adolf Rickenbacher with the original "frying pan" at his home in Fullerton, California, 1974.

Nature and Independence
Mari Sandoz (1896–1966)

In 1884, when Jules-Ami Sandoz (1857–1928), aged 27, arrived in frozen Sheridan County in the northwestern hills of Nebraska, the land was still mostly available for pioneers to settle. Even if his first winter there proved to be particularly devastating, it reminded him of the snows of his home country, the highlands of the Swiss Jura. Older than the two other young travelers with the same given name (Jules Tissot and Jules Jacot) who had joined him on his expedition back in Neuchâtel (in the French-speaking part of Switzerland), he was given the nickname "Old Jules." It would stick to him throughout his entire life and to this day, since it was his nickname that made him famous.

His first child, Mari, published as her first work a piece of historical fiction that made of her father an emblem for the conquest of the west and won her a place among the privileged 100 specialists in the field. Admittedly, Mari Sandoz had more than enough material for a brilliant novel: the man was extravagant, stubborn, ill-tempered, a womanizer, a braggart, a clever fighter, a stamp collector, a postman, an abortionist, a dealer in medicines, ammunitions, guns, horses, gas, cars, a prize-winning grower of pears and apples, an impresario of Sunday night balls and a limping grumbler. Where others wanted to raise stock, he decided to grow orchards. When most immigrants feared the Indians, he became their close friend. Establishing new-comers on unclaimed land and registering them became his main occupation. He expected such an awesome future for his adopted homeland that he managed to convince dozens of European immigrants, including several members of his own family, to settle in the Sandhills, as they were called. When his father, the veterinarian Ami-Frédéric Sandoz, came to Nebraska for a visit in the early 20th century, he was puzzled that six of his seven children (as well as all of his brothers and sisters) had chosen to establish themselves in this arid and harsh country, away from the cultural life they were used to: they didn't even have a proper bathroom! But if Mari Sandoz's three brothers and two sisters did lack a good scholarly education, Old Jules had been right about their prospects. Some twenty years later, Little Jules, James, Fritz, Flora (married to Boris Kicken) and Caroline (married to Robert Pifer) were the proprietors of five big ranches, each one with a herd of cattle numbering more than 1,500 head. The five ranches together were bigger than the Swiss canton they had come from. On these High Plains, with their hunters, cowboys and Indians, the frail but resolute Mari Sandoz was the only one to choose a literary career, but she did so with the help of an extraordinary temperament and an iron will.

Witness to the conquest of the west

Sophisticated east-coast publishers at first showed no interest in the little lady from a remote region full of uneducated cowboys. The manuscript of *Old Jules* was turned down 14 times before it was finally published, going on to receive an award from the *Atlantic Monthly* and to be chosen as the November 1935 selection of the *Book Guild.* Metro-Goldwyn-Mayer would buy an option for the film rights of the book for $25,000. *Old Jules* turned out to be a huge, instant popular success, and it was at this point in her career that Mari Sandoz showed she had the talent of a major writer.

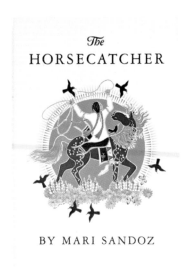

The
HORSECATCHER

BY MARI SANDOZ

MARI SANDOZ
THE BEAVER MEN

Old Jules By Mari Sandoz

Afterword by Helen Winter Stauffer

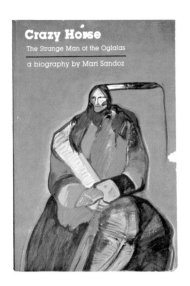

Crazy Horse
The Strange Man of the Oglalas
a biography by Mari Sandoz

Mari Sandoz

Sandhill Sundays
and Other Recollections

Introduction by Virginia Faulkner

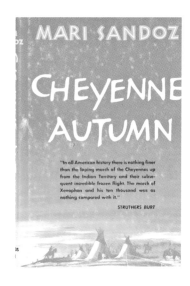

MARI SANDOZ

CHEYENNE
AUTUMN

"In all American history there is nothing finer
than the loping march of the Cheyennes up
from the Indian Territory and their subsequent incredible frozen flight. The march of
Xenophon and his ten thousand was as
nothing compared with it."

STRUTHERS BURT

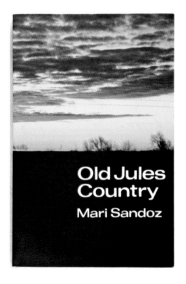

Old Jules
Country
Mari Sandoz

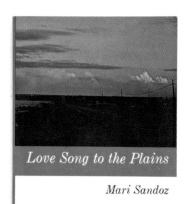

Love Song to the Plains

Mari Sandoz

Her subsequent work, including some thirty novels, biographies, essays and short stories, would remain true to the region of the High Plains where she had spent her youth. She demonstrated great skill at documentation and researched each one of her subjects at length and with extreme care. Her study was filled with thousands of notes, from which she drew the material for her stories. She spent months documenting her subjects, interviewing all possible sources, and traveling to the remotest locations for additional information. She excelled in depicting the life of the settlers, never hesitating to denounce scandals and frauds. In *Slogum House* (1937) she depicted the life of a woman avid for power with such reality, with scenes of such shocking sexual context, that the Mayor of Omaha banned the book from state public libraries. Another controversy followed with the publication of *Capital City* in 1939, an exposé of fascistic tendencies in the politics of Lincoln, the state capital. By taking up an anti-war position in *The Tom Walker* in 1941, she drew violent criticism from those who thought her stance during the Second World War lacking in patriotism. Mari Sandoz turned a sharp eye on the misdemeanors of her society, championing the poor and oppressed as well as adopting clearly feminist and ecological views with immense determination.

In defense of the Indians and nature

Above all, Mari Sandoz was an ardent defender of the Indian cause, and in this she was unique among North American authors. She invested herself in the defense of the Indians with unheard-of resolve at a time when the U.S. government still seemed more or less bent on eliminating them. She wrote four books on the subject,

all of them masterpieces. Praised for its fast-paced action and beautiful language, *The Horsecatcher,* published only in 1957, was her first novel about the Indians she knew so well. Without ever leaving the world of a Cheyenne tribe in the 1830s, she created a youthful protagonist many readers will recognize in themselves. Young Elk is expected to be a warrior, but it sickens him to kill so much as an enemy. He would rather catch and tame the wild mustangs that run in herds. His determination to be a horsecatcher will require a moral and physical courage equal to that of any warrior, and while he must earn the right to live as he wishes, he must also draw closer to family and community.

Crazy Horse (1942), a biography of the Sioux chief, is well researched and depicts Indian life with such accuracy that it certainly contributed to the fame of the strange man of the Oglalas. The biography demands the reader's admiration as Mari Sandoz gets her audience to see through the eyes of Crazy Horse, vividly revealing the tragic fate of his tribe. It is an initiation into Indian culture, into the native way of life, and it goes so far as to allow the reader to enter into the subtleties of the Indian language.

In *Cheyenne Autumn* (1953), Mari Sandoz recounts the epic 1878 flight of a Cheyenne tribe from its Oklahoma reservation, and its journey to its homeland in Montana, 1,500 miles away. It is a gaunt, bloody, heroic story, achieving a powerful eloquence in the final chapters, evoking as they do the courage to face death. This time the story caught the attention of Hollywood producers, and no less a director than John Ford brought it to the screen. Shot in 1963 with a star-studded cast unusual for a western, including Richard Widmark, Caroll Baker, James Stewart, Sal Mineo, Dolores del Rio and Edward G. Robinson, *Cheyenne Autumn* is considered John Ford's most humanitarian film, thanks no doubt to the author's compassion for the Indians' fate.

The Battle of the Little Bighorn (1966) is the last major book published by Mari Sandoz. For many critics, it constitutes both her best work and the richest narrative of General Custer's last battle. Once again the author gathered extensive documentation of the fatal expedition, and once again she manages to adopt the point of view of both the white men and the Indians; this time, however, the book reads like a thriller. Its structure makes plain the inexorable pattern drawing its heroes towards the final catastrophe: the death, at the end of June 1876, of Custer and close to two hundred of his men.

The Sandhills of the High Plains of northwestern Nebraska remained in Mari Sandoz's heart her whole life long. She depicts their flora and fauna as well as the lives of hunters, trappers and fur traders with a rare talent, in books like *The Buffalo Hunters* (1948) or *Love Song to the Plains* (1961), a lyrical salute to the earth and sky. In *The Beaver Men* (1964), however, she set herself a higher goal: covering more than two centuries, the book ranges from the beginning of the beaver trade along the St. Lawrence in the 1630s to the last great rendezvous of traders and trappers on Ham's Fork, in what is now Wyoming, in 1834. While her focus is on beaver hunting, the cumulative effect of the study is much broader than a conventional historical examination. Her essential concern is ecological, the relations of living creatures with each other and with their physical world. It is this perspective, unique among chronicles of the fur trade, that gives the book its very considerable value. The treatment of the role of the Indians, too, is a good deal more complete than in most studies.

The Mari Sandoz Heritage Society

A self-educated bibliophile as a young woman despite her father's prohibition against the reading of novels, Mari Sandoz obtained a third-class certificate in 1913 allowing her to teach in rural zones. Her younger brothers and sisters as well as some neighborhood kids were her class. At the age of eighteen she married Wray Macumber, only to divorce him four years later and establish herself in Lincoln, where she studied at the university and first felt the urge to write. From then on, her life would merge with the subjects of her books. She lived for a few years in Denver before taking up residence in New York, which would remain her home

until her death in 1966 at the age of seventy. She was by then a renowned writer, quoted in the encyclopedias and read in schools, and three of her works are listed among the hundred most important books about the conquest of the West. She has been inducted into the Nebraska Hall of Fame and visitors can admire a memorial drive on the grounds of Old Jules' farm. In 1971, The Mari Sandoz Heritage Society was created at the college of Chadron, in northwestern Nebraska. One building on the campus has recently been turned into the Mari Sandoz High Plains Heritage Center, housing both her archives and a permanent exhibition on her life and works, as well as being devoted to the investigation of the history and culture of the High Plains.

Literature

Jelmini, Jean-Pierre et al. (eds.), *Les Sandoz: une famille des Montagnes neuchâteloises à la conquête du monde,* **Hauterive 2000.**

Sandoz, Mari and Stauffer, Helen W., *Letters of Mari Sandoz,* **Lincoln 1992.**

The Mari Sandoz Heritage Society's archives, Chadron.

Non-fiction (selection)

Sandoz, Mari, *Old Jules,* **Boston 1935.**

Sandoz, Mari, *Crazy Horse: The Strange Man of the Oglalas,* **Lincoln 1942.**

Sandoz, Mari, *Cheyenne Autumn,* **New York 1953.**

Sandoz, Mari, *The Buffalo Hunters: The Story of the Hide Men,* **New York 1954.**

Sandoz, Mari, *The Beaver Men, Spearheads of Empire,* **New York 1964.**

Sandoz, Mari, *The Battle of the Little Bighorn,* **Philadelphia 1966.**

Novels

Sandoz, Mari, *Slogum House,* **Boston 1937.**

Sandoz, Mari, *Capital City,* **Boston 1939.**

Sandoz, Mari, *The Tom Walker,* **New York 1947.**

Sandoz, Mari, *The Horsecatcher,* **Philadelphia 1957.**

Illustrations

P. 98 **Mari Sandoz at the Van Fleet Ranch, Colorado, 1947.**

P. 100 **Selected works of Mari Sandoz.**

P. 101 **Film version of** *Cheyenne Autumn* **(1963), dir. John Ford.**

P. 102 **Mari Sandoz in her Hudson Street apartment in New York City, 1930, in the background a map of Nebraska.**

P. 103 **Mari Sandoz with the Levi Strauss Golden Saddleman Award she received from the Western Writers of America for her book** *The Horsecatcher,* **1963.**

P. 104 **The Mari Sandoz Heritage Society, 2005.**

Science and Foresight
Fritz Zwicky (1898–1974)

Looking back at his life, Fritz Zwicky wrote of his ancestors and himself: "It was our aim to serve our world and our homeland by being loyal to the place we lived while acting as citizens of the world."

Fritz Zwicky was the scion of an old and distinguished family from Mollis in the canton of Glarus. His great-grandfather and grandfather before him had also escaped their narrow valley and spent many years abroad. As for his father, Fridolin, he had been sent to work for a local textiles manufacturer at the age of 18 in Constantinople, now Istanbul, before moving to the port town of Varna on the Black Sea. He went on to set himself up there as a merchant and small manufacturer, marrying a young woman from Bohemia. And so it was that Fritz Zwicky and his younger siblings Rudolf and Leonie were born in Bulgaria.

But while his father and siblings spent virtually their whole lives in Varna, save their last years, at the age of six Fritz was sent to his grandparents in Glarus, where he attended primary and secondary school. As one of his classmates was to put it decades later, "Fritz Zwicky was ahead of us all in knowledge and intelligence. He excelled in all disciplines." He wrote the best essays, was a master at both French and drawing, and was also a fine gymnast and stenographer. Mathematics was in his blood, and he was particularly fascinated by physics. So it was not surprising that the 16-year-old Zwicky was not forced to follow in his father's shoes. He attended industrial college in Zurich and graduated with the highest marks ever attained by a student there.

He then went on to study mechanical and electrical engineering at the Swiss Federal Institute of Technology (ETH) in Zurich before preparing to take a teaching degree in mathematics and physics. It was during this period that he became friends with the math and physics lecturer Hermann Weyl, and attended guest lectures by Albert Einstein. At the same time he was politically active, observing the doings of Lenin and "other Communist agitators at close range." In the summer of 1920 he graduated with a 5.45 out of 6, a result he proudly noted was more than half a mark better than that achieved by Einstein 20 years earlier at the same university.

He then worked for four years as an assistant at the ETH's physics institute, doing his doctoral work with Peter Debye and Paul Scherrer. In his spare time he went on lengthy mountain hikes, mostly together with the future Nobel prize winner for medicine, Tadeus Reichstein.

Gazing at heaven

Zwicky's life took a decisive turn in 1925. That was the year that the President of the Rockefeller Foundation visited the ETH with a companion. Zwicky showed the two of them around, and at the end of the tour they asked the young scientist whether he would like to come to America on a fellowship from the Rockefeller International Education Board. Would he ever! Asked what his dream destination was, Zwicky replied, "Where there are mountains." The three quickly decided on the California Institute of Technology in Pasadena.

Thus Zwicky came to the United States, the beginning of a long and successful career as a scientist. The story goes that among the first things Zwicky asked Robert A. Millikan, President of Caltech, was whether there were any good climbing mountains around. "Can't you see them," asked Millikan, pointing to Mt. Wilson, almost 6,000 feet high. *"Ja,"* grumbled the Swiss alpine enthusiast, "I see the foothills."

Zwicky received a warm welcome at Caltech. He felt right at home in the intellectually challenging atmosphere of the university, surrounded by a host of renowned researchers, and was soon promoted to assistant professor. Over time his interest shifted from solid-state physics to astrophysics. And while his theories met with scanty acceptance among his conservative colleagues, he was celebrated by the general public.

During Albert Einstein's half-year stay in Pasadena, the *Scientific American* reported, in March of 1932, "Dr. Zwicky's name was mentioned frequently among those of the best-known scientists in the course of cosmological discussions." Professor Einstein was said to consider him one of the "most promising young physicists." A few months later, he was described in the magazine *Fortune* as "an alpine climber, a collaborator of Einstein's and one of the most brilliant theoretical physicists at Caltech."

That same year he married a young woman from Pasadena society, Dorothy Vernon Gates, the daughter of a California senator. After eight years of childlessness, however, the marriage was to falter, and ended soon after in divorce.

Zwicky's contribution to science consists in the discovery and study of countless heavenly bodies. In the 1930s and 1950s in particular he was often to be found at the Mt. Wilson and Mt. Palomar observatories in California. In 1933, together with the prominent astrophysicist Walter Baade, he developed the theory that supernovas are formed by the implosion of ordinary stars, and that they set loose such tremendous quantities of energy that they glow one hundred times more brightly than an entire galaxy.

Zwicky calculated that one ought to discover four supernovas a year, and indeed, between 1937 and 1939, with the help of the comparatively tiny 18-inch Schmidt telescope mounted in a small dome on Mt. Palomar, he observed twelve. Back home in Switzerland, too, notice was taken of these first-ever supernovas, with even the *Neue Zürcher Zeitung* running a story under the headline "The Zwicky Super Nova," an unusually personalized title for the otherwise staid newspaper.

Throughout it all, Zwicky remained an enfant terrible, both in sports and in science. He built a ski jump on Mt. Palomar and is said to have jumped more than 50 feet. On the basis of his observations of nebula clusters and his thinking about them, he astonished scientists with proof that the universe was unable to expand. Furthermore, flying in the face of contemporary scholarly consensus, he showed that it had taken much longer for the individual galaxies to achieve their current distribution.

Over the course of his career as a researcher he discovered a total of 123 supernovas. Many heavenly bodies bear his name, including faint blue or Humason-Zwicky Stars, as well as dwarf galaxies in Sextans and Leo (Zwicky Systems). The structures listed in his important astronomic catalogs (1961–71) are known as Zwicky Galaxies and Zwicky Clusters. The compact galaxies he discovered turned out in the mid-sixties to be quasars, or quasi-stellar radio waves.

He was a welcome guest at international meetings throughout the 1950s and 1960s, where his lectures bubbled over with ideas: new theories, the search for supernovas and compact galaxies, the "space race" and the possibility of human activities on the moon. His crowning moment came in 1973 in London when Sir Fred Hoyle, President of the Royal Astronomical Society, presented him with that distinguished institution's gold medal and spoke warmly of his achievements.

A new life after the Second World War

Immediately following the end of the Second World War, Zwicky was sent to Germany by the commander of the American air force, General H. H. Arnold. He was to gather information on the findings of German scientists and technicians involved in the V2 program, known as "Unternehmen Peenemünde" after the place where the rockets were produced for the bombardment of England. Arnold was so impressed by his report that he sent him on a follow-up mission to Japan with orders to study and document the effects of the American atom bombs. His conclusions, however, were ignored.

In 1947 Zwicky worked for three months as an adviser to the technology section of the Swiss federal military department. His aim was to shake up the Swiss defense establishment with his experience in the U.S., Germany and Japan, but he enjoyed only modest success. During this period he met the 18-year-old Margrit Zürcher at a hotel, married her on the spot and took her with him back to Pasadena. She bore him three daughters and helped out for many years in the evaluation of his astronomical data.

As the scientific director of the Aerojet rocket company (from 1943 to 1949), Zwicky was importantly involved in making improvements to booster rockets as well as to fuels and engines. A total of 16 patents were registered in his name, including those for underwater jets and so-called terrajets, which could propel themselves through the earth. He collected numerous research findings in his *Morphology of Propulsive Power* (1962), which he published at his own expense.

Twelve days after the Russians launched Sputnik, on October 16, 1957, he was able to fire the first human-made object into space from the tip of a rocket built by Aerojet: a tiny sphere, measuring approximately one centimetre in diameter and dubbed "Artificial Planet No. Zero." From then on he was to develop plans for research stations on the moon. In 1976 he was inducted into the International Space Hall of Fame in Alamogordo for his outstanding contribution as a pioneer of space travel.

In his quest for all manner of rocket fuels and engines, Zwicky created what he called the morphological box, essential to his system of morphological analysis, the method of thought and action he developed. Morphological analysis is a universal method for systematically finding a solution to almost any problem.

No less a figure than Gottlieb Duttweiler, the founder of Switzerland's renowned Migros supermarket chain, engaged Zwicky in 1960 for a morphological analysis of his company. Other Swiss companies hired him as well, including BBC, Escher Wyss, Heberlein, CIBA and Bührle/Contraves. Morphology has since become a standard element in the methodology section of any management seminar.

Popular even with "the stupidest of all peoples"

The many lectures he gave after the Second World War, at such places as the ETH and the Migros-Klubschule, a popular night school run by the supermarket chain, made a celebrity of Zwicky in Switzerland as well. His three books – *Morphologische Forschung* (Morphological research, 1959), *Entdecken, Erfinden, Forschen im morphologischen Weltbild* (1966, published in English as *Discovery, Invention, Research through the Morphological Approach,* 1968), and an eccentric autobiography, *Jeder ein Genie* (Every man a genius, 1971) – were also popular successes. His referring to the Swiss as "the stupidest of all peoples" (because of their failure to take advantage of their opportunities) did, of course, stick in many craws.

Fritz Zwicky made a splash outside the scientific arena as well. He was an active citizen who lived publicly, making no distinction between his research and his private life. He always said what he thought, whether to his colleagues, the authorities or in private, true to his belief that honest people value honesty. This meant that he fell into disfavor in some circles, and was barred from entry into others. But there were also those for whom his undaunted stand against hierarchies, nepotism, party hacks and losers was a shining example.

When the McCarthy era had reached its hysterical nadir in 1955, Zwicky was ordered to seek American citizenship or be denied access to secret projects. Zwicky resolutely refused, maintaining that "a Swiss head needs to stay on a Swiss body!" As a result, his security clearance was canceled and he was barred from his own projects.

Since his student days he had been an advocate of peace, freedom, democracy and decentralization, no hollow words but a mission, whether in the world of politics or of science. He championed public discussion and international cooperation, prudence and modesty. He thought of himself as a "Free World Agent of Democracy." It was his conviction that every single human being and every single people represented a kind of genius, with talents and special gifts. And he believed that these talents and gifts should be taken advantage of, in a spirit of constructive criticism, in order to build a "decent organic society." He felt that it was the duty of each person to help to create a world in which everyone could live, a "more peaceful world equipped with gentle and organic means of propulsion and sources of energy."

Upon retirement he began to toy with the idea of returning to Switzerland. A few friends, seeking to prepare the ground for him, attempted to secure him research work and created the Fritz Zwicky Foundation in Glarus. Their plans were foiled, however, by Zwicky's untimely death on February 8, 1974, in Pasadena.

Fritz Zwicky was enormously versatile. As a person he could come on strong, but he had a warm heart. He was as clear sighted as he was stubborn, which made him an uncomfortable figure for many. He was ahead of his time, and he was often proved right in retrospect. Over 500 publications, now preserved together with his comprehensive handwritten literary estate and book collection in the Glarus cantonal library, testify to Zwicky's productive fervor.

Tributes to his life and work may be found in the *Brockhaus Enzyklopädie*, the *Encyclopaedia Britannica* and Paris's *Encyclopaedia Universalis*. In 1979 *Meyers Enzyklopädisches Lexikon* even went so far as to call him "one of the most important astrophysicists of the 20th century."

Literature
Müller, Roland, *Fritz Zwicky: Leben und Werk des grossen Schweizer Astrophysikers, Raketenforschers und Morphologen*, Glarus 1986.
Syrek, Tammy Ann, "Zwicky, Fritz (Feb. 14, 1898–Feb. 8, 1974), Astrophysicist," *Dictionary of American Biography,* supplement nine, 1971–1975, 1994.
Trudel, Jean-Louis, "Zwicky, Fritz (14 Feb. 1898–8 Feb. 1974), Astrophysicist and Space Scientist," *American National Biography,* vol. 24, 1999.

Illustrations
P. 106 In 1937, with the help of the comparatively tiny 18-inch Schmidt telescope, Fritz Zwicky discovered the first supernovas.
P. 109 (l.) Fritz Zwicky with his wife Margrit at the light box they used to evaluate astronomical images, c. 1965.
P. 109 (r.) Fritz Zwicky at the California Institute of Technology in Pasadena, 1971.

Politics and Log Cabins
Yule Kilcher (1913–1998)

Yule Kilcher had a vision, and he remained true to it throughout his life: he wanted to lead a simple existence with like-minded people, in harmony with nature and as self-sufficiently as possible. He was convinced that the ability to do without material things was intimately connected with an inner spiritual abundance. In order to lead such a life, Kilcher left his native Laufen, in the canton of Basel-Landschaft, in 1940 and, at the age of 27, struck out for Alaska. Together with his wife Ruth Weber, a young woman from Pratteln in the same canton, and their eight children, Kilcher, whose ancestors had come from the Schwarzbubenland region of the canton of Solothurn, would go on to farm more than 600 acres south of Anchorage. Over the course of several years he also got involved in politics, and, even after all of his children had left home and he had parted from his wife, continued to cling with characteristic stubbornness to his vision of the simple life. When Yule Kilcher died at the age of 85 in 1998, Alaska's flags flew at half-mast to honor this man who had grown to such prominence in the northernmost American state.

In the lonely regions of Alaska

At the age of 16 or 17, Kilcher, who had been baptized Julius Jacob but would come to be known as Yule, set out to walk and hitchhike through Europe and North Africa. From carpenters in Sweden and the Carpathian Mountains he learned how to build log cabins, and began to formulate his plans for emigration. Interviewed in the 1984 documentary portrait *Die schwierige Schule des einfachen Lebens* (The simple life: a school of hard knocks), Kilcher described the origins of his philosophy in a family that had always been at odds with the world, and had a great taste for history and politics.

He traveled to Alaska for the first time in 1936, only to return to Switzerland three years later in search of the small group of companions who had wanted to share with him the simple life in the great north. To his great disappointment, however, he now found that none of them was ready to make good on their initial promise, and he broke definitively with his old home for a lonely future in Alaska. In 1941, Ruth Weber, seven years his junior, followed him there, and, although they barely knew each other, they were married on the spot. They felt their shared ideals provided them with sufficient common ground for a life together.

The couple's unconventional lifestyle was also reflected in the names they chose for their children. Their eldest daughter Mairiis was born in 1942, followed one year later by Wurtila and, in 1945, the year the family moved to Homer, south of Anchorage, Fay. Five more children were born over the next years, three girls (Sunrise in 1949, Stellavera in 1955, and Catkin in 1958) and two boys (Attila or "Atz" in 1947 and Otto in 1952).

Homer's climate is comparable to that of the foothills of the Swiss alps, at an altitude of almost 5,000 feet. The summers can be warm with cooler periods and the winters are snowy and cold, although the temperature seldom falls below five degrees. The family farmed, gathered berries and mushrooms, hunted game in the local woods and fished in the nearby sea. They cooked and heated with hard coal from a seam in the seaside cliff outside their house. Every now and then Yule's brother Edwin, who had grown wealthy in South

America, would send the family a little something. It was a life of relative isolation from their closest neighbors, packed together in a small log cabin without electricity or running water. If you wanted to be alone you had to go outside. They whiled away the long evenings with games, music-making and singing. Until the school bus started to make its runs near enough to the Kilcher homestead, Ruth home-schooled the children – in High German, as she was later fond of pointing out.

In the limelight

Yule and Ruth were both musically gifted, and passed on their love of music to their children and grandchildren. Jewel Kilcher, AKA Jewel, Atz Kilcher's daughter, played in bars with her parents from an early age, singing and yodeling and learning the ropes as an entertainer. Today, Jewel is a celebrity in the U.S. Her first album, *Pieces of You,* appeared in 1995 and sold more than 10 million copies. "Foolish Games," the single, was a number one U.S. hit in 1997. In January 1998 she had the honor of singing the national anthem at the opening of the Super Bowl. Currently (according to her website), following a three-year creative break, Jewel is about to release her eagerly-awaited sixth album, said to be her most personal production to date.

The astonishing success of the blonde with U.S. and Swiss citizenship, whose undeniable talent is by no means, however, unique, must be ascribed to the hardnosed marketing campaign conducted by her record label. A Swiss journalist who interviewed her for the magazine *Facts* in 1997 wrote that Jewel had provided the U.S. music industry with the big star it so urgently needed as it struggled with eroding sales figures. She looks good, seems complex (by turns serene and naive), her background is eccentric and slightly exotic, and her ballads do no one any harm. Her grandfather Yule is supposed to have praised her beautiful voice while having nothing but contempt for show business.

As for her father Atz, he sees his daughter only every now and then, living as she does in the sunnier south of the United States. Sometimes she calls to tell him whom she's just met or been to lunch with. He's impressed, he says, and openly admits his pride in his daughter in his mix of Basel and Solothurn dialect with a strong American accent. He goes on to say that he had thought her success would do something for his own music career. The music teacher from Homer has already recorded several albums and still sings regularly in clubs

and bars, but his CD sales and performance bookings aren't all he had hoped for. Jewel's aunts also think she could give her father a helping hand, at least by having him open for her once.

While Jewel continues riding on the back of her success, other Kilchers are enjoying their own moment in the limelight. Q'orianka appears in Terrence Malick's latest film, *The New World,* in the role of Pocahontas. It's the first big break for the 16-year-old, the granddaughter of Wurtila, the second-eldest of Yule's daughters, who now works in a Waldorf school in Southern Germany. Jewel has now been a celebrity for more than ten years, no mean feat in the fickle U.S. music business, and it will be interesting to see whether Q'orianka makes out as well.

Communicative visionaries

If there was one thing that Yule and his children were good at, it was producing themselves in front of an audience, talking up ostensibly trivial matters and getting people to believe them. Sunrise Kilcher recalls with mixed feelings how she and her siblings were made to stand at attention. "Instead of just being allowed to lead our lives and have our feelings in peace, it seemed to me at the time that we were only doing these things so they could be recorded for posterity," she told the director of *Die schwierige Schule des einfachen Lebens,* Alfi Sinniger, in a taped interview. "That really emptied the experience out, as well as making it very frightening." It's true: Yule Kilcher did indeed document the growth of his family and their daily experiment in living practically from the very first, on 16-mm film, just like a pro.

After the war, the Kilchers made regular trips to Switzerland to show their films and slides. Atz was born in Switzerland in 1947, and Catkin, who is now a Lieutenant Colonel in the U.S. marines stationed in Hawaii, was born there in 1958. Today there is a whole series of films by and about the Kilchers, including *A Pioneer Family in Alaska,* which has made it into the archives of the Smithsonian Institution in Washington. Stories like theirs, from the period between 1862 and 1986 when settlers were able to acquire and farm property on the legendary "frontier" under the Homestead Act, are a central part of the (white) national American identity. It was pioneers like these who built the U.S. into the giant it is today, and public interest in their histories and biographies remains accordingly high.

Yule Kilcher was not content to simply stay on his property and live out his ideals in private. He had a vision, and he wanted to share it with the world. It was easy for him to reach people, regardless of where they came from or what they did, no matter their social position. Dixie Belcher, an old friend of Yule's, recalls that the many visitors to his homestead included German millionaires, Hollywood producers and Cambodian priests. Yule was fond of debate and impressed his listeners with his broad learning, wide reading and intelligence. What could be more natural for a man like that than to get into politics?

In the mid-1950s he was one of 55 delegates to the Alaska Constitutional Convention, which met from November 8, 1955, to February 6, 1956, near Fairbanks to draft a constitution for the future state. "Yule Kilcher," reported the *Anchorage Daily Times* on December 12, 1955, "[is] a farmer from Homer who would rather split theories than logs and who thinks the city slickers at the convention need some spurring. ... Kilcher wears a wool shirt, weather-beaten canvas parka and yellow rain hat to the proceedings."

The minutes taken over months of talks are filled with Yule's name. He was an alert presence during the extremely complex negotiations, speaking up often and arguing with equal parts intelligence and stubbornness. Many of his votes were as unconventional as his appearance, for instance when he championed calling the administrative districts of the new state of Alaska "boros" rather than "boroughs." "I don't see any reason at all," he argued, "why we should stick to this u-g-h spelling. It hasn't changed since Chaucer used it. It has a nostalgic reference looking back towards New York and further beyond the ocean towards England. ... America has always been modern in changing the English spelling ... and [also] in order to alleviate the school children's spelling in the future ... a change of spelling I think would be welcome." But the old spelling prevailed, and is manifestly still in use to this day. In April 1956 the new constitution was adopted in a referendum, and three years later Alaska became the 49th State of the Union.

Kilcher sat in the State Senate from 1963 to 1967, where he was mainly involved in environmental issues. He watched with the greatest dismay as his beloved Alaska was pulled ever deeper into the maelstrom of civilization, and lamented the dreadful effects of the exploitation of its natural resources, particularly its oil, on its natural fabric and the human beings who lived with and from it.

In 1969, after nearly 30 years together, Yule and Ruth Kilcher got a divorce. Ruth could no longer see a future for herself in Alaska and started a new life in Tennessee with Rod Mariott, a former U.S. army officer. Yule remained in Homer, living on in the old house where he had raised his family. After the divorce Ruth went to work as a journalist, writer and translator. She had already written during her time in Alaska, having been President of the Alaska Press Women and Regional Director of the National Federation of Press Women in the 1960s. She had kept a diary since she was a girl. In the 1980s she published two volumes of poetry, one in English, *Voice of an Initiate,* and one in German, *Strömen im nieversiegenden Strom* (Flowing in the never-ceasing current). The books are a testament to her profound spirituality, her closeness to nature and her sympathy for anthroposophy. In 1997, a few years after Ruth's death, the Pratt Museum in Homer and the Homer Society of Natural History produced *The Rich and Simple Life: Remembrances of Homesteader Ruth Kilcher.* The video, which contains footage from Yule's early films, extracts from Ruth's diary and interviews with their children, is an homage to Ruth as well as to all of Homer's homesteader women. The title come from a story Ruth wrote in 1938, in which she foretells her life in Alaska.

In Alfi Sinniger's film, Atz Kilcher talks about his parents, and about the difference between them: "I could sense my father's restlessness and his constant feeling of not achieving what he had set out to achieve, always needing to get something else done. He always thought he was too late, and I never had the sense that

he was having fun. With mother I could tell that she was enjoying [her life]. She was happy whether she was planting flowers, picking berries or gathering mushrooms. She was calm and relaxed, she would whistle and sing. I felt that my mother liked doing what she did. Father, on the other hand, had a dream, a goal. He used to fire up the people around him, get them to help him make his dream a reality."

Without a doubt, Yule Kilcher had the ability to enthral people and fill them with enthusiasm for his ideas. In the eulogy printed in the *Juneau Empire* on December 9, 1998, one day after Yule's death, a life-long friend testified to this gift: "He sure impacted the lives of everyone who met him by force of his personality. He had a tremendous life force." Many were the companions on his journey, bound to him by their curiosity and by their love. For his part, he remained true to himself his whole life long.

Literature and films

Sinniger, Alfi, *Die schwierige Schule des einfachen Lebens,* Topic Film, 1984.

Wüest, Markus, "Yule Kilcher: Von Laufen nach Homer, Alaska," *Basler Zeitung,* 15.03.1999, number 62, p. 2.

Zipperlen, Helmuth, "Ein Siedler, Politiker und Visionär, Yule Kilcher – ein Solothurner Auswanderer prägt Alaska," *Solothurner Zeitung,* 24.11.1999, p. 21.

Illustrations

P. 112 Ruth and Yule playing the flute.

P. 114 Yule and Ruth plowing, before 1947.

P. 115 The young Kilcher family: Ruth and Yule with Mairiis, Wurtila and Fay.

P. 117 Growing family: Yule, Sunrise, Wurtila, Atz, Ruth, Fay and Mairiis.

Ambivalence and Longing
Robert Frank (*1924)

I doubt the world-famous photographer and artist Robert Frank would call himself an immigrant to the U.S. And he certainly wouldn't say he was an *emigrant,* although he would have more grounds to do so. Born into a Jewish family in 1924 in the Enge district of Zurich, he only received Swiss citizenship in March of 1945, as it were when it was already too late. His father, an importer of Swedish radios, watched the progress of the Second World War from the family's uncertain refuge in Switzerland with accordingly heightened concern; indeed, with understandable fear.

From Albisgüetli to New York

"When the war was over" – this phrase has a special resonance for European photographers. It is the very motto of an unparalleled explosion into the world. Swiss photographers in particular, as Willy Rotzler said of the Zurich Concrete Art movement, had experienced the five and a half years of war as a time of incubation. Somewhat older colleagues, such as Paul Senn, who had documented the Spanish Civil War, and Werner Bischof, founding member of the international photo-agency Magnum, took off immediately, to war-torn Germany first, and then to the U.S. and Latin America. Only Hans Staub remained behind in Switzerland, along with Jakob Tuggener, whose center was both a studio and a sort of alchemist's cabinet. "The war was over and I wanted out of Switzerland. I didn't want to make my future there. I found it too closed in, too small a place," Frank recalled in a 1986 conversation. The first destination for "young folk" like René Burri or his older contemporary Frank was Paris. The chairs in the Tuileries were made to dance once again, this time through Hans Finsler's lens, only now there was something of the postwar melancholy about them. But the real attraction now was the New World, more than a century earlier acclaimed as a fountain of youth by Heinrich Heine.

The long period of incubation had given rise to a longing for distant places, an unquenchable thirst for the "American way of life" with its promises of a new freedom. An entire generation had caught the bug. It had been carried by Free Jazz, the perfect expression of a boundless individualism, by the lyrics of the Beat poets, and by films and plays, like Thornton Wilder's *The Skin of Our Teeth,* which Frank saw performed in German at Zurich's Schauspielhaus theater in 1944.

Frank arrived in the U.S. for the first time in 1947 at the age of 22. He had boarded the S.S. *James Bennett Moore* on February 20 and landed at Ellis Island in March. He wrote to his parents immediately: "This is truly a free country. You can do what you want. No one asks to see your papers." His immigration documents have not been published, and it is possible that they are among the creatively heaped stacks of paper in his wooden fishing hut in Mabou in Nova Scotia, waiting to be made into collages or to serve as material for a film. Such official documents have always been important to Frank. After all, they provide at least bureaucratic proof of his existence, so often mislaid in reality.

Nevertheless, his relationship with the United States remained ambivalent for some time. "I don't think I will stay here long. Everything moves so fast, and you're always just one of 8 million people here... The only thing that matters is money," he wrote to his parents in November of 1947. From 1949 to 1953, therefore, after the sudden end of his fashion job (shooting for *Harper's Bazaar*) and a trip to Peru and Bolivia in 1948, he traveled regularly between Europe and America with his wife Mary and their son Pablo. He went so far as to write to his parents on February 28, 1953: "I am going back to New York for the last time now, to try to get to the top on the strength of my own work." But he was in the end to stay on, and the fact that he did so, and that he did soon achieve a measure of fame, is perhaps due to his relationships with photographers like Walker Evans and Edward Steichen – as well as, of course, to his own talent.

The Americans

In his application for a Guggenheim Fellowship on October 11, 1954, a step that would have great consequences, Frank described himself as a "naturalized American," although he was not to receive U.S. citizenship until October 18, 1963, without ever renouncing his Swiss passport.

From that point on he referred to himself as possessing double citizenship, and he is often described as a "Swiss-American photographer," despite his undoubted preference for a reversal of the hyphenated terms. He was over the moon. "Dear folks," he wrote to his parents, "I have never experienced so much in one week as I have here. I feel like I'm in a movie. Life here is totally different from Europe. Nothing counts but the particular moment; no one seems to care about tomorrow."

With his Guggenheim, Frank was able to undertake the trips necessary for *The Americans,* the photo-essay he finished in 1957 but which did not appear, with Delpire in Paris, until 1958. What might be considered his artistic tribute to the country in which he was living had been held up by the controversy surrounding its unvarnished realism and the novelty of its formal approach. Finally published in New York in 1959, with an introduction by Jack Kerouac, the book contained precious views of everyday life in the 1950s. On the reverse of a draft of the book Frank had written "America, America" as well as "I am an American."

He was extremely grateful to the U.S. institutions and friends from whom he had received help, including the art director at *Harpers,* Alexey Brodovitch, whom he has revered ever since and whom he thanks in virtually every exhibition and photography book; two Guggenheims; Jack Kerouac and Allen Ginsberg; the American artist June Leaf, his second wife; and the National Gallery in Washington, to which he donated his early photography archive and which, in 1994, devoted to him its first ever retrospective of the work of a living photographer.

When he and June Leaf moved to the Canadian town of Mabou in 1971, to a lonely house on the Nova Scotia coast, without, however, giving up their place at 7 Bleecker Street in Manhattan, it signaled the end of a crisis nearly ten years in duration, a period he had nevertheless been able to occupy with film-making. Withdrawing from life in the big city and the art scene there allowed Frank to focus on his late work, a primarily autobiographical oeuvre that was heralded in 1972 with *Lines of my Hand,* as well as to gain some distance from a country that was increasingly abandoning its ideals to a crude faith in the blessings of power and money. And, as life-long leftists (without any special partisan affiliation), June and Robert were comfortable with the authentic, easy-going quality of life in the Canadian countryside.

During the years of his American success and crises, Frank had been considered a difficult person by his Swiss contemporaries in particular, despite film productions with Ruth Waldburger, exhibitions with the

Swiss Photography Foundation, collaborations with *du* magazine, the cultural journal, and many close friendships in Switzerland. Now, engrossed in his autobiography, he began to think more and more about his Swiss (and Jewish) roots. He started visiting more often, and not merely his old friends the graphic artist Werner Zryd, the banker Fernando Garzoni, George Reinhardt in Winterthur, and Walter Binder of the Swiss Photography Foundation. The rapprochement seems to have been sealed by two marvelous donations to the "Photofoundation" as well as by the Zurich publisher Walter Keller's production of re-editions and catalogs with Scalo.

When I visited him in New York recently, however, the tide seemed to have turned once again. As if to signal this, he welcomed me into his kitchen on Bleecker Street waving a report on the front page of the *New York Times* in which the Swiss authorities were taken to task for their treatment of the Austrian Jews who had just been recognized as the heirs to paintings by Klimt. Despite its merely tangential Swiss connection, the piece had provided him with the excuse to fulminate bitterly against Switzerland for its refusal to learn from history.

"I'm a Switzer lad and I love my land"

And yet he has been back since, not only to heal his battered knees and feet on a tour of health resorts from Schinznach to Ragaz but also to see his wife June's show at the Tinguely Museum in Basel and to visit that same Jura scenery whose depiction by the painter Charles l'Eplattenier graces the wall of his kitchen in New York.

His roots in the Enge district of Zurich doubtless have a great deal to do with this, his parents' abandoned apartment, the Enzenbühl cemetery, the Albisgüetli fairgrounds, the number 13 tram. He has meditated on these memories in recent films *(Moving Out, The Present)* and expressed the desire for his celebrated exhibition at Zurich's Kunsthaus in 1995 to be followed at Winterthur's Fotozentrum by the recent retrospective *Storylines,* which had been at the Tate Modern in London; and he has talked about a special advance run of publications in Switzerland.

And while it used to be at most a few photographs of the Albisgüetli, a Mayday demo in Zurich or early contact sheets that would make it into books and exhibitions, we can now see his outstanding 1949 pictures of a meeting of the Hundwil local assembly. In 1941 and 1942, between apprenticeships with the photographers Hermann Segesser and Michael Wolgensinger, Frank worked as a still photographer on the Swiss feature films *Landammann Stauffacher* and *Steibruch,* during which time he made his own contribution to the "intellectual national defence" of Switzerland, a notion popularized by the 1939 National Exhibition that had taken place practically next door to his parents' home. He was also an enthusiastic boy scout, skier and mountaineer. *"Ich bin ein Schweizer Knabe und hab die Heimat lieb* [I'm a Switzer lad and I love my land]," as he wrote with a certain irony to a friend from back home in 1990, playing on the lyrics to a patriotic song from his childhood.

Frank's roots were nurtured in that Swiss childhood and youth – a period part natural paradise, part political menace, part Jewish urbanity whose product was in equal measures claustrophobia and familiarity with normal, everyday life, and thus surely the fertile ground from which has grown his entire oeuvre. His first teacher, the "craftsman" Hermann Segesser, also has a great share of responsibility for his success. As for Frank's technique, that was refined later on in contact with his master Wolgensinger, himself a former pupil of Finsler's, as well as in collaboration with the Eidenbenz Studio in Basel. He developed his "eye" for life on the

street by studying Arnold Kübler's *Zürcher Illustrierte* and the many excellent pieces published in it; beginning in 1941, he could also learn from Kübler's *du* magazine. On film sets he got to know the anti-fascist resistance, as personified by Leopold Lindtberg and Sigfrit Steiner.

So his sweeping account of the American people, as published in *The Americans,* first-rate both as an artistic work and as a sociological document, is greatly indebted to the Swiss "soil" out of which Frank grew. This does not mean, of course, that Frank's work will not continue to be praised as a "contribution to America," a brilliant piece of American visual culture and 20th-century history.

His place, between big America and little Switzerland, thus remains one of ambivalence. Perhaps Frank is simply another Jewish citizen of the world, an urban type that exceeds the frame of national reckoning. Unfortunately, his family was forced to learn in the most personal fashion the extent to which nations can intervene in personal destinies, an experience that left him deeply affected, skeptical and forever cautious to judge. As for his teaching, it is without a doubt that which the truth of his own life has conveyed to him: elsewhere.

Literature

du – Zeitschrift für Kultur. Robert Frank, vol. 11, November 2002.

Frank, Robert, *The Americans, new edition,* Scalo, Zurich 1993/1998.

Frank, Robert, *The Lines of my Hand, new edition,* Scalo, Zurich 1989.

Greenough, Sarah and Philip Brookman, *Robert Frank: Moving Out,* National Gallery Washington 1994, Scalo Zurich 1995.

Stahel, Urs et al. (eds.), *Essays über Robert Frank,* Winterthur 2005.

Illustrations

P. 122 Robert Frank's photographs get top prices on the international art market.

P. 123 Robert Frank at the opening of "Paper Route," an exhibition on the Arteplage Mobile du Jura, Expo 02, in Yverdon-les-Bains, August 2002.

Erika Hebeisen

Death and Defiance
Elisabeth Kübler-Ross (1926–2004)

In 1969, while a man was landing on the moon, a woman was successfully challenging the taboos surrounding death and dying. It was a typical Wednesday during term, and a large group of medicine and theology students, nurses, religious caregivers and social workers were attending a university lecture in the auditorium of Chicago's Billings Hospital. The woman at the lectern was the physician and psychiatrist Elisabeth Kübler-Ross, and she was engaged in a dialog about dying with a 22-year-old woman suffering from leukemia, shielded behind two-way glass. What do patients think about as they await their own death, she wanted to know. How do relatives and hospital staff deal with their anger, their fears and their hopes? It was a typical Wednesday, except that today a journalist and a photographer were also present at the "death seminar," and the resulting seven-page article, published on November 21, 1969, in *Life* magazine, brought Elisabeth Kübler-Ross instant fame. Her renown as a pioneer researcher into the phenomenon of mortality was further established by the virtually simultaneous appearance of her book *On Death and Dying,* which went on to become a best-seller. It was translated into 26 languages and earned its author a slew of honorary doctorates.

While her research into the taboo area of death and dying shook society, Kübler-Ross also made possible a range of therapeutic approaches not coincidentally first crowned with success in the United States. American universities were attracting a host of innovative researchers throughout the 1960 and 1970s, drawn by the opportunity to develop unconventional methods and explore fields unknown to science. What is more, there was also a large and enthusiastic audience for such research. Kübler-Ross was one of these ambitious young scientists: in just ten years, the insignificant Swiss immigrant, who had arrived in the US with nothing more than a state medical degree, was famed as a researcher into death and dying. In an afterword to Derek Gill's 1980 biography, Kübler-Ross wrote: "My destiny had to be the United States, where I was free to pursue my own work, my own research and my own form of teaching, none of which would have been possible in any other nation in this world. Here, through this teaching, through my own methods and my owm enthusiasm and belief in my own work, not only with dying but with so-called hopeless schizophrenics and with blind and retarded children, I finally found home."

At home and on her own

Elisabeth Kübler was born one of triplets in 1926 in Zurich. As she never tired of recalling, she weighed scarcely two pounds at birth, and her chances of survival were not thought to be great. And yet the Kübler triplets flourished, growing up together with their elder brother in an upper-middle-class Protestant home in the city of Zurich for the first four years of their lives, before moving to the nearby lakeside community of Meilen. As a child Elisabeth felt most at home in the natural surroundings of this more rural family residence, as well as, eventually, in the mountains, where her father would take her hiking, and taught her how to ski and rock-climb. And then there was the "Fürlegi," an alpine chalet above Amden. This was to become her affective home, the site of what might be called her political awakening. It was here, far from the everyday world, that she encountered a group of activists from the International Voluntary Service for Peace, whose account of the battlefields of the Second World War aroused in her a desire to enter that world, as well as the will to bring it material and moral healing.

Before she was able to join the efforts to rebuild a war-ravaged Europe, Kübler-Ross had a battle of her own to fight – with her father, who had already planned her education as a clerk. The 16-year-old was faced with a choice: either yield, or strike out immediately on her own. She chose independence. With her mother's help she organized a year in the French-speaking part of Switzerland, an established custom in those days for well-born young women. She left her position there after months of exploitation and humiliation at the hands of the lady of the house and began to seek a vacancy for a lab assistant, in order to fulfil her dream of working as a physician in Africa or India. Her Polish-Jewish supervisor at Zurich's University Hospital, where she underwent training, helped her make her first foray with the International Voluntary Service for Peace. She was to take part in its reconstruction projects a total of five times between 1945 and 1947, in France, Belgium, Italy, Sweden and Poland.

When she had completed her studies she went on to work as a lab assistant at an eye clinic, where she also found a mentor, the specialist Marc Amsler, who regularly allowed her to return to her job following each of these field assignments. At the same time she was attending evening courses to prepare for her school-leaving exams, which she passed in 1951. She then went on to register for medical school at the University of Zurich. Towards the end of her studies there she applied for a six-month stint in a research project in India, but was turned down soon after receiving her degree in the fall of 1957. At the same time, however, her American fellow student and fiancé Emanuel Ross was urging her to accompany him to the U.S., and, although Kübler-Ross was not especially keen to go, she decided to marry him and emigrate, half-heartedly at first, to the United States.

Migration and integration

The just-married couple boarded the *Liberté,* a steamer, in the French port of Cherbourg in June of 1958. Kübler-Ross would have sour memories of the crossing: neither the excellent food nor the sun or evenings of dancing on board could counteract her feelings of ambivalence "about leaving Switzerland for a country I had no interest in." Upon arrival in New York the couple took a one-room apartment on 96th Street and found positions as assistants at the Glen Clove Community Hospital, which Kübler-Ross left in the summer of 1959 for work on the psychiatry ward of Manhattan State Hospital. Although she wrote of the ward's nightmarish quality in her diary and referred to it as an insane asylum, Kübler-Ross found her first professional challenge there in the form of care for forty chronically schizophrenic women, and within two years she had managed to re-integrate a significant number of her patients. She reduced medication, removed restraints, created incentives to work and found external care opportunities. Her method included the use of individual therapy sessions, which she was later to enshrine at the heart of her research into dying: she was able to get "hopeless" patients to speak, and she gave them someone to speak to. During this period Kübler-Ross and her husband had moved to a three-room apartment in the Bronx, where in the summer of 1960 their son Kenneth was born. Two years later Kübler-Ross completed her training as a psychiatrist.

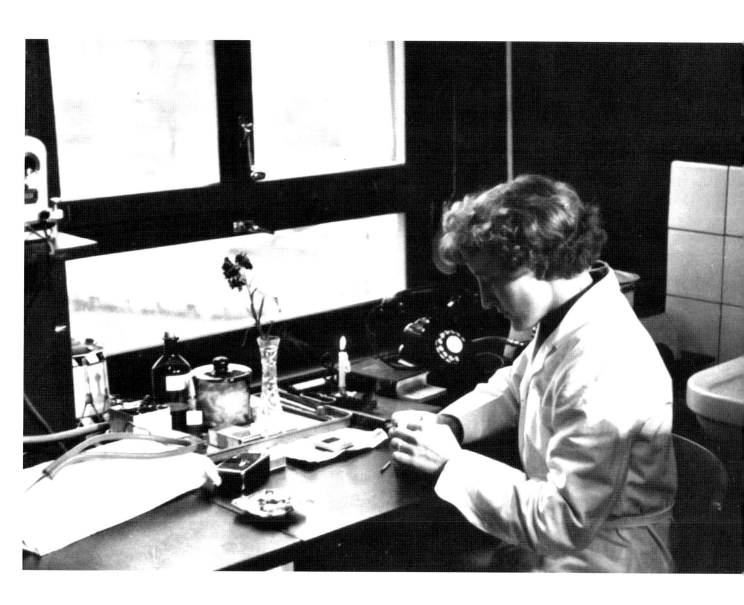

Through her family and her profession, Kübler-Ross was also being integrated into American culture. She wrote to her mother in Zurich, "I really feel at home now in America, and have taken on some of the traits I was so critical of at first. For example I now enjoy going to the supermarket, I like hamburgers, hot dogs and packaged breakfast cereal. You will be glad to know that I haven't started chewing gum yet! But don't let it upset you too much that I wear pants as often as dresses now, even when calling on people." Before her breakthrough as a researcher into death and dying, Kübler-Ross was to bend to her husband's professional aspirations twice more. Their daughter Barbara was born in 1963 in Denver, where the family was living in a detached house. As she confided to her diary at the time, "Although I will always be thankful for my Swiss heritage, my emotional connection to Switzerland has grown so weak that it would cause me no pain to break it altogether. I truly feel more at home in America than in the country of my birth." At the University of Colorado, Kübler-Ross also discovered the research subject that was to occupy her for the rest of her life: her first lecture was about cultural and clinical methods of dealing with death.

Researching and accompanying the process of dying

When Kübler-Ross moved once again with her family in 1965, this time to Chicago, and accepted a position as psychiatrist at Billings Hospital, she was confirmed in her observation that doctors and nursing staff were not only engaged in the attempt to prevent their patients from dying, they were also doing their utmost to avoid being confronted with death. The hospital, it turned out, a place filled with dying people, was dominated by a particular taboo on death. It was in this environment that Kübler-Ross developed her three-part "death seminars." These involved her first talking about an aspect of dying before carrying on an exchange with a terminally ill patient, and concluded with the students discussing the interview.

Since she had come to prize the dying as founts of knowledge, she wanted rising physicians to take the greatest possible advantage of their wisdom. Her professional colleagues, however, were skeptical, although the patients themselves were glad to take part. Some physicians refused her access to the dying, while others maintained that no one died under their care. The greater the popularity of her seminars, the more vehemently her colleagues rejected her. The hostility reached a peak when the Life article appeared in 1969 and made Kübler-Ross's "death seminars" a media event. The physicians feared for Billings Hospital's image, and were no doubt also envious of the success of Kübler-Ross's On Death and Dying, the book in which she used her many interviews to develop a theory concerning the last phase of human life. She identified five stages between diagnosis and death: denial of the threat to life; anger at fate; bargaining for a last chance; depression; and, finally, acceptance of the unavoidable. She also spoke out against the notion of death as an absolute end. Kübler-Ross used a butterfly to symbolize her view of dying as a transition, a symbol she had first encountered as a 20-year-old at the concentration camp Majdanek, one of the sites of systematic muder and of millions of deaths. Carved into the walls of the children's barracks there she found hundreds of butterflies.

Work and influence

Her renown as a researcher secure, Kübler-Ross left Billings Hospital in 1970. She continued to work with dying children in another Chicago hospital as demand for her lectures grew, until she was traveling some

200,000 to 250,000 miles annually and speaking each week to audiences of up to 15,000. At the same time, released from institutional restrictions, she was developing a workshop on "Life, Death and Transition" that was intended to convey her message on a more individual level. The workshop, first held with some 60 people in rural Indiana, involved focusing her thoughts on dying more closely on the process of life itself. Later, as demand for it increased, especially in the 1970s and 1980s in the U.S., Canada, Australia and much of Europe, Kübler-Ross was forced to limit enrolment for the one-week event to 100.

Kübler-Ross was becoming ever more interested in what came after death. She approached this subject by studying near-death experiences and was a pioneer in the creation of the interdisciplinary field known as thanatology. Meanwhile she was also ranging farther afield in her quest to uncover the secret of life after death. Beginning in 1977, her Shanti Nilaya center in the Escondido hills in southern California hosted a series of encounters with alleged healers promising a glimpse of eternity. This flirtation with esoterica was short-lived, however, as Kübler-Ross was in the end more interested in practical methods to ensure a dignified death. Eva Bacher-Kübler recalls how proud her sister was of her contribution to the hospice movement. The first American house for the dying was founded in New Haven, Connecticut, and in 1977 the doors of the Elisabeth Kübler-Ross Hospice were opened in St. Petersburg, Florida. Just one year later Kübler-Ross, who was by then on the board of numerous such institutions, could look back on over fifty more opening days. By the end of the 1970s, however, her passionate commitment to the demystification of death and her championing of a more humane approach to dying had exacted their toll, and her marriage with Emanuel Ross foundered.

The early 1980s saw Kübler-Ross setting out once again on a new voyage of discovery. Moving to the east coast of the U.S., she turned to the fight against AIDS and opened Healing Waters, a 300-acre farm devoted to offering courses and therapy. Her project for a hospice to house twenty babies with AIDS was defeated by the local population; instead, Kübler-Ross established an adoption service, finding by her own account homes for 350 ailing infants. Her book *AIDS – The Ultimate Challenge,* published in 1987, portrays AIDS as a paramount threat to human society. And yet she was not widely supported in this new campaign where she was living, something that Kübler-Ross took quite personally. In 1994 her home on the Healing Waters property burned to the ground, and, although arson seemed likely, no one was ever charged with the crime. She had lost not only a piece of property but her books as well, her research archives, her correspondence and her personal souvenirs, such as gifts and diaries.

Kübler-Ross spent the last phase of her life near her son, in the remote seclusion of the Arizona desert, where she was tied to her bed and wheelchair by a series of strokes. Despite her longing for death, she would never have hurried its advent: Kübler-Ross's own taboo was assisted suicide. She even refused to help her mother in such an undertaking, although she had been completely paralyzed (but compos mentis) for the last four years of her life. But what would she have made of Terry Schiavo, the case that aroused so much controversy in America in 2005? She might well have supported her assisted suicide: after all, Schiavo had been in a coma for 15 years and was only continuing to exist with the help of machines. At the same time, Kübler-Ross was forever warning doctors against "playing God" with patients who were still capable of expressing their feelings. What is certain is that Elisabeth Kübler-Ross had helped make it possible to hold a debate about assisted suicide in the first place. Two years before her death, in 2002, a documentary film, *Dem Tod ins*

Gesicht schauen (**Looking death in the eye**) gave a poignant insight into Kübler-Ross's own encounter with dying. Here, one last time, is the Kübler-Ross we know from her books and lectures, the energetic, far-sighted researcher driven by a sense of her own mission. The only difference is that now, in old age, the familiar twinkle in her eye has come to seem like wisdom.

Literature and films

Gill, Derek, *Quest: The Life of Elisabeth Kübler-Ross,* New York 1980.

Haupt, Stefan, *Dem Tod ins Gesicht schauen,* Frenetic Films, Zurich 2002.

Kübler-Ross, Elisabeth, *On Death and Dying,* New York 1969.

Kübler-Ross, Elisabeth, *AIDS – The Ultimate Challenge,* New York 1987.

Kübler-Ross, Elisabeth, *The Wheel of Life: A Memoir of Living and Dying,* New York 1997.

Illustrations

P. 127 Elisabeth Kübler-Ross in the lab, late 1940s.

P. 128 Elisabeth Kübler-Ross on her Healing Waters farm in Virginia, 1987.

Blues and a Bit Out of Place
Walter Liniger (*1949)

He's the perfect American: graying, gangly, moustache and jeans, steering his shopping cart with one hand through the supermarket, with the other hand twitching sweet potatoes out of the pile and snagging a caffeine-free Cola from the shelf. Everything done easily, every casual gesture, sunglasses pushed up on his head riding high behind a hank of his hair. He mumbles instructions to the butcher as he passes, tells him he'll pick up his spare ribs on the way back, the whole thing drenched in the local slang. Only the miniature Swiss railway watch on his wrist and the cantonal coat of arms on the rear of his dented old van outside in the parking lot identify him as the railway-man's boy from the Länggasse district of Bern. As well as the railway ties he uses to terrace the garden of his row-house on the edge of the forest.

Walter "Wale" Liniger, born in 1949. He worked as a secondary-school teacher over there in Kehrsatz, Switzerland. Here in Columbia, South Carolina, he professes the blues at the University of South Carolina's Institute for Southern Studies, because he knows the history and anecdotes of the southern states better than the natives. Before that, from 1984 to 1992, he developed the blues archives at the University of Mississippi in Oxford, Miss., interviewing scores of musicians and documenting the local culture, a foreigner in the heartland of the blues. When he was a high-school student back home, he was once expelled from music class because Mr. Schläfli disapproved of his performance in Haydn's "Creation". It was the blues that gave him the courage to return to music later. On his most recent CD, *Better Day,* he's on his own, a motherless child, except for the parts where he's accompanied by the friend who's like a mother to him, Etta Baker, born in 1913 in North Carolina and probably the world's oldest professional musician.

He's a teacher, a musician – and a student

Driving north on the interstate to see his Etta, Liniger never has both hands on the steering wheel at once: he's constantly gesturing, putting his palm flat on his belly, tapping on his left breast over his heart and saying things like, "The blues is when you bring yourself into your music." He thunders on the entire trip, his deep, booming professor's voice heavy with significance as we pass through four hours of faceless back country, past identical tracts of single-family homes, trailer parks and gas stations. He broods continuously. "Blues is loneliness, it's having no one to blame but yourself." All this in the pungent Bernese dialect he has by no means lost in his years abroad, but rather cultivated. It gives his utterances a down-home flavor, like something out of the 19th-century Bernese novelist Gotthelf, as he develops parallels between now and then, his new home and his old, comparing the farm life of his ancestral Sumiswald with the Mississippi Delta and Gotthelf's hero Uli, a tenant farmer, with black southern sharecroppers, who continued to be exploited even after the end of slavery. "The aim of capitalism," he says, likening the dastardly plantation owners of old to modern credit institutions, "remains the entanglement of the poor in a web of debt." And he's back to the blues, this time in our own era, just the way he presents it in his college courses. "Young people don't understand the language of the blues anymore, filled with references to pickaxes, mules and wheelbarrows. But if they learn to interpret blues metaphors, then it becomes highly relevant. Then 'stubborn mule' suddenly means 'stupid computer.'"

The blues? Music in code, complaining but never accusing, because it provides its own consolation. The blues, with its twelve-bar structure the originary source of all popular music. Of course, Liniger doesn't simply introduce the blues to his students as the venerable tradition of the first Afro-Americans, based on West African rhythms and the pentatonic scale and later taken up by slaves and oppressed black sharecroppers in the U.S. south to give vent to their own troubles. Liniger starts by teaching them how to play the harmonica and thus illuminates a whole socio-cultural context for them, sensitizing them to their own political present-day. Or he has them read the memoirs of a Vietnam vet, "to show them the damage done to people by war. I teach them to think outside the mainstream." He confronts his students with unexpected, uncomfortable ideas. "What's the best thing about Hurricane Katrina," he asks, and is met with silence. He answers his own question: "That America has finally seen the face of poverty, which is not confined simply to New Orleans but exists in every major American city." His blues courses are courses in life. "I teach them to pay attention. 'Illegal worker' is a term making the headlines at the moment in the U.S. But who is it who gives these so-called illegal people work? It's precisely the same folks who wrap themselves in the flag and vote for Bush!" It's incredible that he can get away with this in conservative South Carolina. "Just think," he says, surprised himself. "They had the courage to give an outsider a job talking about their own culture."

Liniger is always both at once, musician and teacher. Some people are bothered by the fact that his concerts are always also history lessons, and he claims it doesn't faze him. *"He, nu,"* he says in Bernese, *"de halt,"* which means essentially, "Take me or leave me." "Blues is about finding your own natural voice." That's what he learned from the Delta blues singer James "Son" Thomas, his dark and distant mentor for nine years until Thomas's death in 1993, the man he made *Gateway to the Delta* with, winning the W.C. Handy Award, the greatest prize in the blues business.

Thomas and Liniger, the odd couple

It was a mini-sensation that the pale-faced "son of Switzerland" and the black-skinned "Son" Thomas ever got together at all, because you'd have to be wearing some pretty rose-tinted glasses to believe that black and white actually co-exist in today's southern United States. Liniger was the first recipient of a blues fellowship in Mississippi, a so-called "apprenticeship" from the National Endowment for the Arts. Of course it was only $2,000, and two-thirds of it went to his master, "Son" Thomas, while the rest was spent on gas. But it gave rise to an artistic relationship that saw the two of them going on tour together, holding workshops at schools. Thomas with his guitar and his voice, and Liniger with his blues harp: an odd couple. Liniger himself says of the duo, "What you had was a middle-class foreign intellectual together with an illiterate from the oral tradition. It was the first time ever that a black blues musician was playing with a white man in Mississippi. It was a difficult time, but it taught me a great deal. Thomas helped me to experience the mystery of the blues, its macabre side." And of course also its doubts, its anger and depression. "It wasn't until I met Etta Baker that I rediscovered my pleasure in the music."

And there she is now, in her Nikes, jeans and knitted sweater, sitting in front of her tiny three-room house in Morganton, the place where she raised nine children, and grinning all over her wrinkled face. Like every day,

she got up at four this morning to put wood on the fire in the kitchen and straighten up the garden. She has a dozen birdhouses out there, as well as places for her dog and her cats to sleep. And now here it is, not yet lunch and there's time for a little music-making. She gets out her Gibson electric, vintage 1958, the way other old ladies take out their knitting, and starts to playing bluegrass, ragtime and folk. Her fingering is amazingly light and adept.

Liniger comes in on guitar and harmonica while Baker, caught up in the collaboration, rocks back and forth, sticking out her chin and drawing it back in, occasionally pulling a cheeky little stunt with the neck of her guitar like a rock star, beaming all the while like a mischievous little girl caught with her hand in the cookie jar. Music is this old lady's photo album, her treasure chest, her diary. When she plays "Dew Drops," her first song, learned at the age of three on her daddy's lap, it's as if her father had come back to life. For 90 years now Etta Baker has made music every single day, a way of immersing herself in memories of her loved ones. Mostly all by herself at home.

Liniger comments: "All the old people I have spoken to about the blues connect it with memories. The blues is a mental process that puts you in touch with your past. It doesn't work for me that way, however, because I don't have any memories of my childhood that are associated with the blues." Only very few Americans (and no Europeans) have studied the blues as profoundly as he has. And yet he has never come to feel totally at home in the tradition. "The blues have given me a lot, but they will never be able to awaken the feeling of home in me. It remains for me an individual experience." That's why in his performances he often segues from a blues number into a Swiss folksong, like "Chumm, mir wei ga Chrieseli gwinne" or "Im Aargöi sy zwöi Liebi." It's a way of building a bridge to his own memories, to a communal feeling.

Etta Baker, the maternal friend

When Etta Baker shows up in town she is met with cries of "Hello, mother!" She gets the same greeting at the Sagebrush Steakhouse, a greasy spoon with dark wood walls that looks like a saloon from a spaghetti western. What style of music does she play? "Home-made music," says the great-great-grandmother, taking a bite of her cheeseburger. It's something of an understatement. Her Piedmont blues and her very own guitar technique, known as southern finger picking, are legendary, and her parlor is festooned, alongside yellowing landscapes, photos of her descendants and pious mottos, with numerous prizes from foundations, cities,

national awards as well, including the proclamation of her National Heritage Fellowship, signed in 1991 by President George Bush, senior. At the reception in the White House she met B. B. King and Ray Charles. "B. B. was very nice," she says, "but Ray was an arrogant twerp." And she can hardly talk about the pilgrimages made to Morganton by celebrities like Taj Mahal, looking to learn her guitar stylings, without giggling. She finds any kind of fuss embarrassing. The oldest musician in the U.S. gets invitations from all over the world, but she will only go to places she can reach in one day's journey. She'll get into her vintage Buick with the crack in the windshield and putter off to a folk festival. As a young girl she used to play dance music, until, so the legend goes, her husband Lee forbade her, jealous of her beauty. Of course he liked to live the high life himself while she toiled in a textile plant to make ends meet for her family. It wasn't until after Lee's demise in 1967, hard upon their 17-year-old son's death in Vietnam, that she started appearing again, and she made her record debut in 1991 at the age of 78.

A life full of secrets. Her ancestors were not all Afro-Americans: there was an Irish great-grandmother too, as well as native grandparents. Her everyday life, meanwhile, is a tribute to her Cherokee heritage, even if she won't say why she plants medicinal herbs by the light of the full moon. When she doesn't want to answer a question, Etta Baker simply hums a resonant falling-and-rising "mmh, hmmm," the sound southerners make when they need to keep their distance while remaining amiable. While he was on the road with "Son" Thomas, Liniger discovered that the cold war pitting blacks against whites was far from over, in spite of the best efforts of political correctness. And yet Baker let him into her family. First a sinister father figure, then the 'good mother.' "Those two are like night and day," he says. "Thomas was full of negativity, while Etta simply spreads good." What she doesn't say is that, as a child, she found out first hand about southern justice, as distributed by a lynch mob she saw in action. The lady has had it hard, but she's just like her music, filled with a quiet joy, gracious and dignified, and humble too. With her, Liniger is gentle, for all that he is accustomed elsewhere to covering up his vulnerability with bravado; with her he has found something to be optimistic about. When they compare notes on rucola, the "European" lettuce she has planted in her garden on his recommendation, Liniger seems happy, an impression he doesn't make anywhere else.

The rolling hills around Morganton are reminiscent of the foothills of the alps, and the local blend of bluegrass and blues is known as "mountain music." So perhaps Liniger feels at home here in part because the place is a little bit like Switzerland. He returns to his native land regularly, to visit his mother in Herzogenbuchsee near

Bern, give concerts and lead workshops for businesspeople, "where I give their brains a good airing out with the harmonica." Top managers like Ulrich Gygi of the Swiss postal service and Benedikt Weibel of the Swiss national railways have participated with enthusiasm.

During an initial trip in the hot summer of 1969 and a second in 1976, Liniger was fascinated, if also confused, by the land of unlimited opportunity. "The next time I wanted to go with a clear head." Liniger quit drinking in 1982, took a three-year unpaid leave of absence from his school – and never came back. "Coming to the U.S. at the age of 33 was like arriving in the world," he recalls. Although Liniger is married to an American and has been a citizen since 1991, he often feels like a stranger in a strange land in both the U.S. and Switzerland, alienated as well as increasingly isolated. "Even though I have now started to think in English, my emotional structure remains that of a Swiss."

He cannot say any longer exactly why he left Switzerland in 1982, but it seems likely that he was escaping from himself. *Better Day* is the proof that he has found himself again. The album is unadorned, clear and out-spoken, relating the story of a life in 53 minutes, the search for a home, the loss of friends, addiction and atonement. "Astonishing how much courage you need to sing about something that has to do with you," says Liniger. He has found the courage not only to sing about himself, but also to admit what he is not.

"Picked no cotton, never pulled no corn, Wasn't born in Mississippi, and I wasn't raised on no southern farm," he sings in "Picked No Cotton."

And immediately segues into the Swiss standard "Luegit vo Bärg u Tal" on his harmonica. His blues are believable precisely because he does not claim to come from the Delta. His very renunciation of the clichéd claim to authenticity makes him authentic. "After 35 years of research I have come to the realization that I cannot understand the blues," he says. "I accept my limits. For the first time in my life I can allow myself to be fallible." Liniger is aware of the fact that this has helped him to produce one of his best recordings to date. Because the blues is the music of failure, of the restrictions placed on human ability.

But has he found a home, or as they say in German, a *Heimat,* something in between your family dwelling and your native land? He is silent for a moment before saying, "There's no word for *Heimat* in American."

CDs
Walter Liniger, *Better Day* feat. Etta Baker, www.bluesprof.com, 2000.
Walter Liniger, *Conversations,* Fun Key, 1993.
James "Son" Thomas and Walter Liniger, *Bottomlands,* Rooster/P-Vine Records, 1989.
James "Son" Thomas and Walter Liniger, *Gateway to the Delta,* 1987, out of stock.
Etta Baker, *One-Dime Blues,* Rounder, 1991.

Illustrations
P. 132 Guitar players and dancers on the street in Memphis, Tennessee, 1996.
P. 135 Portrait of Walter Liniger.
P. 136 Walter Liniger with Etta Baker.
P. 137 Walter Liniger with harmonica and Etta Baker with guitar.

Davos and Hollywood
Marc Forster (*1969)

There are no books about Marc Forster yet; he has only been a public figure for about five years. If you want to know who he is and where he comes from, enter the keywords "Marc Forster" into an Internet search engine and you will be overwhelmed with information, not all of it accurate. For one thing, he is as frequently called "Foster" as "Forster." Sometimes he's Swiss, and sometimes he's German. He is said to have grown up "in the mountains of Graubünden," in Davos or in Klosters, depending on the site.

The best source of data on the successful Hollywood director is the documentary *Von Davos nach Hollywood* (From Davos to Hollywood), by Fritz Muri and produced by Swiss national television. Switzerland is proud of its native son, even if he does hold a German passport. Marc Forster speaks English, High German and Swiss German, although his dialect comes from somewhere around Zurich rather than Graubünden.

A carefree Swiss youth

Forster grew up in a wealthy family in Davos, which in the 1970s had already turned from a farming village into a winter sport resort town, living mainly off tourism as it does today and endowed with its first urban facilities. Marc's father was a physician and the owner of a pharmaceuticals company. Together with his two elder brothers he enjoyed a youth in which money seemed no object, with vacations on yachts and in five-star hotels as well as a luxury home in Davos itself and a country estate near Lucerne, complete with park and swimming pool. When their parents were away, the three boys were cared for by servants.

Marc is said to have sneaked into a cinema for the first time at the age of 12, to see *Apocalypse Now* by Francis Ford Coppola, starring Marlon Brando. At that moment he knew what he wanted to be: a filmmaker.

His brother Peter recalls Marc assigning his playmates roles, telling them which tree to stand behind and when to join in the action. "Marc always said, 'I'm going to make movies. I'm not doing anything else.'" As was fitting for a rich kid, Forster spent six years at Institut Montana, a boarding school in the mountains above Zug, where he met other sons of wealthy parents from all over the world. He has remained in touch with former classmates from the most varied cultural backgrounds, and acknowledges that they have influenced his way of thinking. Despite rumors that he spent some time at Montana scheming to get around the strict teaching staff there, Forster never really got into trouble, shy and absent-minded as he was.

A compulsion from within

A friend from boarding-school days, Carl von Malaise, remembers Forster forever talking about his dream of becoming a director. "It was a compulsion from within." Werner Edelmann, one of his teachers, says young Marc was even ridiculed by his classmates for his faith that he would complete film school in New York and go on to make movies.

But Forster stuck to his dream, although there were many more obstacles in his path than he could ever have foreseen. It began with his family losing its fortune when his father sold his company and invested in some

A L'OMBRE DE LA HAINE

risky schemes. As far as the family was concerned, the financial collapse came out of a clear blue sky. They were forced to sell their house in Davos; they were allowed to take with them a bed and a chair each, and one table for the five of them. "By law we could have taken cabinets as well," says Forster's mother Ulli, "but they were built in, so it was unfortunately impossible." Although there was no longer any hope of financing for his education, Forster successfully sat the entrance exam for the renowned film school at New York University and began looking for a sponsor. He was able to convince some wealthy friends of the family that it would pay to invest in him, and in 1990 Forster moved to New York to fulfil his dream of making movies.

While Forster was away in New York, studying on borrowed funds, his father died of cancer back at home. Not long afterwards, his brother Wolfgang, who was deaf and who had recently been diagnosed as schizophrenic, committed suicide. That same year his grandmother died. Forster had just finished his documentary *Silent Windows,* on the subject of suicide. He describes this period, in which he was constantly being confronted with death on his trips home to Switzerland, as positive and intense.

Living his dream

Hard times were to follow his graduation from NYU. Forster remained in New York, with hardly any work and not enough money to get by. He was sharing a basement apartment with Audrey Brohy, a Swiss friend. Since the place was too small for two beds they were forced to sleep together.

Forster was living from hand to mouth, constantly begging for loans from friends and acquaintances in Europe. He was sometimes so hard up for money for groceries that he had to have it sent to him by courier service. Nevertheless he continued to turn down scripts that did not meet his expectations, refusing thus to muddy his reputation. His mother could not understand this behavior. She was a pragmatist and saw no reason for her son not to have returned home long before, failing which he might at least be earning money in New York by teaching German. A friend with whom he had shared his dreams while at boarding school says he rejoiced when he heard that Forster would rather starve than give up his ambition. In the meantime, Forster was working on smaller projects; looking back he now says those lean times taught him whom he could trust. "Once you're finished with your studies you have to figure out the business in order to develop an eye for who is honest, who can help you get ahead. Some people will promise you the earth and then do

OSCAR 2005: 7 NOMINATIONS

NEVERLAND
UN FILM DE MARC FORSTER

FRENETIC
FILMS

nothing. So I spent those early years running after people, certain that the next day would bring success." He did occasionally have doubts, even fears. "Of course I worried about very basic things when I was out of money and didn't know how I would pay the rent. And I didn't want to hit anyone else up, I already had enough debts. So at those times I did indeed have no idea how I could go on, and that was frightening. But it was less frightening not knowing where my next meal was coming from than thinking that I would be unable to live out my dream."

His breakthrough came in 2000 with the film *Everything Put Together*. On a budget of $100,000 Forster made a film on the subject of SIDS, sudden infant death syndrome. His actors and crew worked for free. It was shown at the Sundance Festival for independent films – and received the "Independent Spirit Award." His success at Sundance opened doors, and he now had an agent to worry about his career. The authors of *Monster's Ball* saw *Everything Put Together* and decided to sign Forster to direct it. They had already asked a few other directors but had been told that the material was unfilmable. The assumption was that the death penalty and racism were subjects unsuited to wide release. Forster felt otherwise, and he made the film with Halle Berry and Billy Bob Thornton as leads. The story of a love affair between a condemned man's black wife and his white executioner was a worldwide success, garnering Halle Berry the first ever best-actress Oscar awarded to a woman of color.

Forster's next film, *Finding Neverland,* the story of the writer James Barrie, was a major Hollywood production. The movie focuses on the friendship between Barrie and the single mother of four boys, the inspiration for his classic children's book *Peter Pan.* He engaged Johnny Depp and Kate Winslet for the leads, with Dustin Hoffman in a supporting role not originally meant for him. Hoffman was simply dying to work with Forster and personally set his hat at the part of the theater director in *Finding Neverland.* At first, however, Forster wanted simply to get rid of him, thinking the role too small for such a big star. What was more, he worried that Hoffman would steal the show by getting all the attention. It wasn't until they talked one to one that Forster changed his mind. "I was sitting there and suddenly I thought, 'Are you nuts? Dustin Hoffman wants to be in your film and you're saying no to him? That's totally insane!'" There followed another hit, with seven Oscar nominations and American film critics voting it the year's best.

Back in Switzerland – always at Christmas

Today Forster is one of the best-known directors in American cinema and is overrun with offers. In 2005 he made *Stay,* a thriller about suicide starring Ewan McGregor and Naomi Watts. His latest picture, a comedy entitled *Stranger Than Fiction,* features Dustin Hoffman, Will Ferrell, Emma Thompson and the rapper Queen Latifah and is due out in 2006.

Forster believed in his dream, and in himself. Despite an untenable situation he remained in the U.S. The fact that he was from Switzerland seemed significant to his teacher Christine Choy at NYU. She noticed that he worked hard and didn't talk as big as many of his American co-students, who were mostly out to make a fast buck and thus fixated on whatever junk the market happened to be calling for. But it takes a real artist, she knew, to get rich making good films.

Forster maintains close ties to Switzerland to this day. His mother and brother still live in Graubünden, and he travels home for Christmas every year. He has also helped out on a Swiss AIDS campaign, and generously

participated in the documentary made about him by Fritz Muri for Swiss national television. Together with the director and his team he re-visited the boarding school above Zug, met with his former teachers and talked about his life. He also provided a glimpse of his current existence in Los Angeles and his work there. Despite his success, Forster does not expect people to recognize him on the street. Not in Switzerland, and certainly not in Los Angeles.

Films
Forster, Marc, *Everything Put Together,* USA 2000.
Forster, Marc, *Monster's Ball,* USA/Canada 2001.
Forster, Marc, *Finding Neverland,* England/USA 2004.
Forster, Marc, *Stay,* USA 2005.
Forster, Marc, *Stranger Than Fiction,* USA 2006.
Muri, Fritz, *Marc Forster: Von Davos nach Hollywood,* Switzerland 2005.

Illustrations
P. 140 Scene from *Monster's Ball,* 2001.
P. 141 (above) Scene from *Finding Neverland,* 2004.
P. 141 (below) Scene from *Stay,* 2005.
P. 143 Marc Forster and Halle Berry after the Academy Awards Ceremony, 2002.

Bittersweet Switzerland

"Everybody talks about the weather," Mark Twain once observed, "but nobody does anything about it." The same might be said about Switzerland as seen by Americans. Curious observers from the United States have been enthralled by their "sister republic" for some time now, and, despite occasional turbulence, relations have remained decidedly cordial over the decades.

From the earliest days, American immigration to Switzerland has only ever been limited and temporary, in stark contrast to the emigration of more than half a million Swiss between 1700 and 2000. There have never been many more than 10,000 American citizens resident in Switzerland, with the last available official figures (from 2001) listing 13,363 "expats," the lion's share in the cantons of Zurich, Geneva and Vaud. So it is impossible to speak of an actual American immigration, although in this regard Switzerland is no different from most other European countries.

All the same, upon closer inspection, three periods of elevated American interest in Switzerland may be discerned. Starting in the 1830s, the first contingent of visitors consisted of selected writers spending a few weeks in Switzerland in the course of their European tours, and penning on the whole intelligent, uniformly benevolent accounts of their sojourn. Industrialization at the end of the 19th century brought businesspeople and investors, focused above all on two archetypal Swiss domains, watchmaking and textiles. Finally, from the 1960s on, U.S. companies began to show growing interest in Switzerland as a site for their European headquarters, what with the low taxes and political stability offered by the country.

William Tell still walks the earth

Switzerland was already seen to possess a special political significance as early as the first years of the 19th century, despite its continuing reputation as the poorhouse of Europe. The most prominent of these early visitors, James Fenimore Cooper, traveled across Switzerland several times and sent home extensive reports. Between 1828 and 1832, starting in France each time, the author of the *Leatherstocking Tales* undertook a number of expeditions through the Bernese highlands and the Swiss interior, to the Lake of Geneva, the Jura and eastern Switzerland. What he saw was a country remarkable for its juxtapositions, its dirt-poor rural communities, largely self-sufficient and evidently not over-endowed with pretty women, as Cooper noted; and then there was Geneva, the enlightened city of Calvin, which awoke his special interest and enjoys the particular favor of Americans to this day. "The Swiss are the only people, in Europe, who appear to me to feel any concern in what has been generally considered to be a crisis in our affairs," Cooper wrote from his lodgings on the Lake of Geneva. Swiss citizens were not only well informed about the political minefield being traversed by the United States, he thought; they were also hoping for a democratic solution to the American crisis, unlike their neighbors, who "are waiting with confidence and impatience for the knell of the union."

Cooper interspersed such meditations with frequent prose landscapes in miniature, a must at the time in any Swiss travelog. And while he was not overcome with the same enduring reveries to which so many travel

writers were susceptible at high altitudes, he weakened in his turn in the face of a Swiss sunset, which he called "The most perfect natural picture I have ever seen." The myth of Switzerland took on added weight since Cooper's accounts of the country, along with those of other authors, were typically published in large editions, and thus had a profound effect on the image of Switzerland as nurtured by the American public. Although he did pay generous attention to its natural attractions, Cooper was also at pains to assess Switzerland's social and political dimensions. After being entertained in Vevey he noted, "The Swiss listened to all this attentively and remarked that America had been much misrepresented in Europe." He came away from a visit to a watch factory persuaded that Switzerland was on the right path, politically and economically speaking (that is, the American path). "The workmen looked intelligent and thoughtful," he wrote, "like men who can both think and do. Some glimpses showed their sympathy with republicanism."

The writer Harriet Beecher Stowe also remarked upon the alpine republic's political kinship with the more enlightened elements in the U.S. She was outraged to see that American slaveholders were touring Switzerland with the intention of justifying their reprehensible activities. "The sophisms by which slaveholding has been justified from the Bible have left their slimy track even here," she fumed. Such behavior not only offended "liberty-loving Swiss," it was also "an insult to the American nation." By her own account, Beecher Stowe received moral support for her anti-slavery campaign from many like-minded Swiss Christians, especially in western Switzerland. For this reason she was inclined to see in the region of Geneva the likeness of progressive New England, while she recognized the American slave states in Switzerland's rural cantons.

Mark Twain, too, was remarkably perspicacious in his assessment when he spent 16 months in 1878 traveling through Germany, Switzerland and Italy with his family, publishing his reactions in the collection *A Tramp Abroad* (1880). Twain's characteristic irony is in full force as he reports on Switzerland, as in his grotesque account of a climb up the Rigi. For him Switzerland is "a large, humpy, solid rock, with a thin skin of grass over it," and it is thus impossible to dig graves here – they must be blasted out of the cliff instead. And yet behind the mischief there is genuine admiration for the beauty of the landscape and the national will to independence. "This is a good atmosphere to be in," he wrote, "morally as well as physically. After trying the political atmosphere of the neighboring monarchies, it is healing and refreshing to breathe in the air that has known no taint of slavery for six hundred years, and to come among a people whose political history is great and fine, and worthy to be taught in all schools and studied by all races and peoples."

Like Cooper, Twain is aware of Switzerland's special place in Europe, and draws parallels between its history and the American struggle for liberation. "There have always been Tells in Switzerland – people who would not bow," he affirmed; and further, "Rütli is a remote little patch of a meadow, but I do not know how any piece of ground could be holier or better worth crossing oceans and continents to see." Of course, such praise must always be read against the unhappy backdrop of Twain's Europe, where he saw for the most part only despots and idiots.

Benefits of a low-wage country

As the experience of a watchmaker and an embroiderer makes clear, Switzerland has also long been a country of unguessed-at opportunity. In 1868, 27-year-old Florentine Ariosto Jones of Boston decided to found a watch factory in Switzerland and export innovative yet affordable products to his homeland. Thanks to its cottage-industry organization and long, hard working hours (factories operated 12 hours a day, six days a week), Switzerland was a low-wage country. Jones had initially planned to base his business in western Switzerland but met strong opposition from the Romands, or French-speaking Swiss, who distrusted the pushy American and wanted to keep their cheap Jura laborers for themselves.

In the end he found a home in Schaffhausen, a city that was on the verge of missing the industrial boat. Recognizing the threat, Johann Heinrich Moser was building the first hydroelectric power station on the Rhine, which would make it possible to operate machinery cheaply and efficiently. Moser joined forces with Jones, and in 1868 they laid the cornerstone of northeastern Switzerland's first watch manufacturing concern, the International Watch Co. The American pioneer summed up his achievement thus: "With the object of combining all the excellence of the American system of mechanism with the more skilful hand labor of the Swiss, we have established our Watch Factory at Schaffusen, Switzerland." But while he may have been a skilled watchmaker, Jones was a wretched businessman, and cash-flow problems forced him to sell the company in 1875. Nevertheless, his motto, "Probus Scafusia" (solid craftsmanship from Schaffhausen) wreathes the IWC brand to this day. Decades later, meanwhile, northeastern Switzerland has been able to profit once again from U.S. investments, this time in the form of med-tech, high-tech and bio-tech companies.

A former workers' neighborhood in the town of Rorschach on Lake Constance features streets named after such American statesmen as Washington, Franklin and Lincoln – and it's all Max Schoenfeld's fault. The clothier, originally a Prussian immigrant to the U.S., had opened a textiles business in Philadelphia before finally settling in eastern Switzerland. In 1872 he traveled to St. Gallen, the world capital of embroidery, to get a piece of that lucrative trade. American women were eager for the fine products, and exports to the New World grew sixty-fold from 1864 to 1880. Schoenfeld and his colleagues built their own factories and patented the Schiffli embroidery machine, thus inaugurating mass production. "The American market seemed inexhaustible," writes Louis Specker in his *Rorschach im 19. Jahrhundert* (Rorschach in the 19th century). "Ever more American buyers appeared, and the mill was supplying exports to the U.S. almost exclusively." The ranks of the employees swelled to 1,800 and the city boomed, enjoying a modern make-over. The German with American entrepreneurial spirit died in 1911, and was thus spared the crisis his industry suffered after the First World War. Although at the time all of the inhabitants of Rorschach mourned him as one, the double emigrant has today lapsed into oblivion. Only the faded inscription "Loeb & Schoenfeld Co." on a wall on 24th Street in Manhattan still recalls the industrial pioneer who did the embroidery business in eastern Switzerland such service.

High-tech and a life of simplicity

Almost a century later, Switzerland is enjoying a roaring renaissance of American interest. Arthur D. Little consultants reckon that 55% of U.S. companies seeking to establish a European base are opting for a Swiss location. Since 2004 alone, Microsoft, Colgate-Palmolive, IBM, Honeywell, Owens-Illinois, eBay, Cisco, Celgen and UPS have all moved their European headquarters to Switzerland, drawn by the same things that attracted travelers in the 19th century: spectacular scenery, a good education system, political stability and (in spite of a certain narrow-mindedness and stolidity) relatively cosmopolitan urban centers. But there is also no point in denying the fact that, without the massive tax breaks the Swiss parliament voted to grant foreign companies in 1997, even Americans would not be coming to the country so readily. Yet while Switzerland is permanently trying to get ahead in the European tax sweepstakes, the controversy surrounding the bio-tech company Amgen's plans to build in Grosses Moos shows that it no longer enjoys the same advantages.

Still, there are also counter-examples, as for instance when U.S. bio-tech Biogen moved its administrative headquarters for Europe, the Middle East, Latin America and Australia to Zug in 2004, and thus came full circle: in 1978 a group of researchers had assembled in Geneva to found the pharma company that would become Biogen. Shortly afterward, of course, Biogen moved once again, this time to Cambridge, Mass., where there are now so many pharma and bio-tech laboratories that Novartis has in turn moved its research base to the U.S. According to the Boston Consulting Group, U.S. companies now employ some 65,000 people in Switzerland, more than 30% of whom hold a university degree, or twice as many as are employed in Swiss firms. After the Germans, therefore, Americans are the second-largest foreign employers in the country.

Ask American expatriates about their experience of Switzerland and you will be overwhelmed with positive responses. Most of them cite the high quality of life as the top boon, especially when compared with the hectic pace of the American everyday. "The secret is simplicity," maintains Bonnie Burns, who left the U.S. for Switzerland at the age of 48, and calls the move a major milestone in her life. "It took me a long time to appreciate the concept that fewer things in smaller places make a life better," she says. For others, however, Switzerland's notorious lack of space poses a problem. "I decided that Swiss people must be blessed with an intuitive grasp of rules and systems, just as they were blessed with magnificent landscapes," recalls Jan Harrington, after a train journey during which her fellow travelers had explained the difference between regional and express trains, as well as the importance of canceling the ticket that one has just paid for.

Catherine Hayoz from Wisconsin also had trouble adjusting when, to her family's surprise, she married a Swiss and relocated to his native land in 1998. At first she found the people arrogant, all too punctual, cold, and orderly, and she suffered from homesickness. But soon enough her idealized image of the U.S. began to wear thin. "Things that used to seem normal now struck me as weird or even unthinkable," she remembers. She was suddenly taken aback by the giant portions in American restaurants, the 12-room homes, the constant barrage of TV ads, the obsession with cars, the violence in U.S. schools. The contrast worked in favor of her adopted country. "I liked it here in Switzerland," she says. "I liked my in-laws, the Sundays spent outdoors, the buses, the food." For all that, however, her final words have a bittersweet flavor: "I still wasn't sure if it was home, but it was here I would most likely spend the rest of my life."

Sources

American Citizens Abroad (eds.), *So Far and Yet so Near: Stories of Americans Abroad,* **Geneva 2005.**

Cooper, James Fenimore, *Residence in France, with an excursion up the Rhine and a second visit to Switzerland,* **Paris 1836.**

Foreign Companies in Switzerland: Joint Study of the Swiss-American Chamber of Commerce and The Boston Consulting Group, **Zurich 2006.**

Twain, Mark, *Mark Twain's Travel Letters from 1891–92,* **Chicago 1892.**

Illustration

P. 146 "Vue du Staubbach" (1837), painting by A. Calame (1810–1864).

Heiner Ritzmann

Swiss Emigration to the United States (1816–1968)
Amerika, Amerika!

As early as the Middle Ages and into the modern era, Switzerland was a major exporter of people, for the most part, of course, to the surrounding countries of Europe. An early estimate has some 25,000 Swiss leaving for North America in the 18th century. There is evidence of an initial large wave of emigrants during the period 1709–1711, followed by further such movements in 1734–1744, 1771–1772 and 1778–1783. These first migrants came from the northern parts of German-speaking Switzerland and were headed for the Carolinas and Pennsylvania, where German immigrants from Württemberg had established settlements. But the French Revolution and the ensuing turmoil on the European continent largely stemmed the streams of emigrants to North America, and they were only to pick up again after the disintegration of Napoleon's empire.

During the century and a half from the Vienna Congress in 1816, which rang in the Restoration, until 1968 and its young people's uprisings, Swiss emigration can be fairly reliably reconstructed, with probably the most detailed figures available for the years 1882 through 1939. At the time, a Swiss federal office charged with the matter assessed the dossiers submitted by emigration agencies and published its findings in the form of annotated annual statistics. For the years 1868 to 1881 the federal government had had to be content with synopses prepared from figures provided by the cantons. Estimates for the period prior to 1868 are based on statistics assembled by the individual cantons, a disembarkation log kept by the Swiss consul in Le Havre, U.S. immigration office statistics as well as information from secondary literature.

After the Second World War, the shipping companies and emigration agencies had to compete with the nascent airlines, which were now making child's play of the once so perilous ocean crossing. The new ease of travel was also a reason for the meteoric increase in reverse migration. While this probably stood at 10 to 15% in the interwar period, according to statistics based on consular reports the proportion of Swiss immigrants to the United States returning to their old homeland had reached almost 70% during the period from 1958 to 1968. With the lackadaisical record-keeping on the part of emigration agencies and the high reverse migration movement, the quality of estimates from the mid-1950s on begins to deteriorate anew.

When they set out

Between 1816 and 1968, some 563,000 people left Switzerland to seek their fortune outside Europe. More than 400,000 of them, or 71.5%, chose the United States as their destination, followed by Argentina and Brazil, in that order.

By far the greatest waves of emigration occurred from 1851 to 1855 and from 1880 to 1884, with the peak of the first period coming in 1854, in which 17,000 Swiss left, and of the second in 1883, with 14,000 emigrants. A brief but intense spurt of emigration in 1816 and 1817 had seen approximately 10,000 Swiss heed the calls to *"Amerika, Amerika!"* The waves that followed in 1845–1848, 1864–1873 and 1886–1893 were of only middling intensity, and the 20th century saw mass emigration solely in the period from 1920 to 1923, although medium-sized waves were documented for 1900–1913 and 1924–1930.

The period from 1816 to 1925 was one in which the Swiss emigration curve underwent enormous fluctuation, due in large measure to the mostly contrasting economic development of Switzerland and the United States during those years. The desolate state of Swiss agriculture was the main driver of emigration in the first half of the 19th century, with a peak in 1816–1817 during the "Little Ice Age" in which the European continent suffered from disastrous harvests and serious flooding, as well as famine in many places. The potato blight, a mysterious fungus that triggered rot and made potatoes inedible, afflicted wide areas of Europe in 1844 and 1845, and Switzerland and other European countries were hit once more by major agricultural crises from

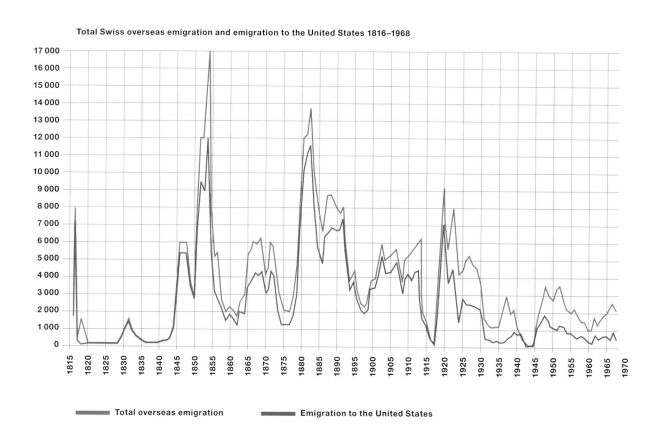

Total Swiss overseas emigration and emigration to the United States 1816–1968

━━━ Total overseas emigration ━━━ Emigration to the United States

1851 to 1855 and again from 1880 to 1884; during this same time the U.S. was profiting from an enduring economic upturn. Meanwhile in Europe, the earlier period had seen a series of failed grain harvests and the lingering effects of the widespread potato blight, while the later half decade was one in which sinking grain prices on the world market ruined countless small farmers.

The sharp dip in emigration from 1917 to 1918 and from 1942 to 1945 may be ascribed to Switzerland's encirclement, during the First and Second World Wars, by warring nations. Emigration picked up quickly between the wars, with agencies organizing departures for almost 10,000 people in 1920 alone. These numbers doubtless included some who had actually wanted to leave earlier, but had been hindered in their plans by global political events. Emigration continued high from 1921 to 1923 as well, driven by the acute postwar depression plaguing Switzerland at the time in contrast to the United States, where the Roaring Twenties were in full swing. The stream of emigrants came to an abrupt halt in 1924, likely due to the effects both of the recovery of the Swiss economy and of the tightening of the quota rules for immigrants introduced in the United States in 1921. These sharpened measures against unregulated immigration also meant that, from now on, total Swiss overseas emigration would no longer run in tandem with Swiss emigration to the U.S.

From 1816 to 1879, three out of four Swiss emigrants were headed to the United States, a proportion that would have been even higher if an Australian gold rush and various settlement projects in Brazil, Argentina and Algeria had not absorbed part of the wave. The fact that some of these ventures ended in spectacular failure, of course, actually led to an increase in emigration to North America, at least indirectly. No less than 83% of Swiss emigrants chose the U.S. as their new home from 1880 to 1913, a figure that dropped to 75% in 1920, to 63% over the next three years and to less than 50% after that. The United States and its neighbor Canada were hit especially hard by the Great Depression of the 1930s, which meant a further drop in the attractiveness of North America for emigrants. The global economy returned to growth in the aftermath of the Second World War, but the age of mass European emigration to America was over for good by that point. Nor was Switzerland any exception to the trend, with Swiss emigration increasing only modestly after 1945 and showing no staying power. Furthermore, in the period from 1945 to 1968, three out of five of these emigrants were headed to destinations other than the United States.

Who they were

The second half of the 19th century saw a fundamental shift occurring in the structure of Swiss overseas emigration, a change in age and marital status as well as in profession and economic status.

From 1845 to 1855, more than a quarter (28%) of the giant wave of emigrants had consisted of married adults, while 42% had been children, which means that, at the time, seven out of ten emigrants were traveling as part of a family. The statistics on age category suggest a tri-generational movement: half of the emigrants were below the age of 20, one third between 20 and 39, and one sixth were at least 40 years old. The contingent of single adult males made up only one fifth of the total wave, while the most common profession was farmer or farm laborer. Contemporary accounts describe virtually all the emigrants as impoverished, some of them in desperate straits. Here and there communities managed to come up with the funds to sponsor the poorest of their members; indeed, on occasion such "emigrants" were actually expelled in organized campaigns.

This mass exodus of needy families during the crisis decade 1845–1855 was not to be repeated. Families already made up less than 50% of the waves of 1864–1873 and 1880–1884, and two out of five emigrants could now be described as "adult, male, single." Poor, impoverished or endangered small farmers continued to make up the bulk of the emigrants from the Old World to the New in terms of professional profile, followed by farm laborers and rurally oriented crafts- and tradespeople. Swiss small farmers were very attached to their rural environment and professional independence, and thus preferred to go overseas than to migrate within their own country, despite the uncertainty and discomfort associated with leaving Europe. With the closing of the American frontier in the second half of the 1880s, however, they were no longer able to pick up arable farmland in the western United States at dirt-cheap prices, and new immigrant Swiss settlers immediately declined in numbers. Statistics by profession assembled by the Swiss federal office of emigration beginning in 1882 show that the share of agricultural workers among emigrants in 1883, a year of crisis, was 64%, but that it had dropped to 38% in 1892 and, by 1900–1930, was holding steady at around 33%. Children also continued to decline as a contingent among emigrants, while people between the ages of 20 and 29 as well as, in particular, single young women emigrated in greater numbers. This last increase was largely due to the booming demand for maids in the United States. As for young male emigrants, they came from the rising trade, banking and insurance sectors, as well as from the mixed bag of "liberal" professions. On the threshold to the 20th century, then, the exodus of the impoverished had been consigned to history.

Swiss overseas emigration by major demographic category 1845–1930 (in percent)

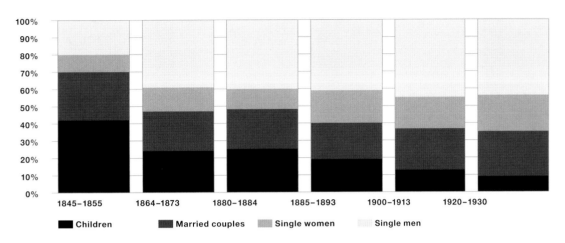

Swiss overseas emigration by age 1845–1930 (in percent)

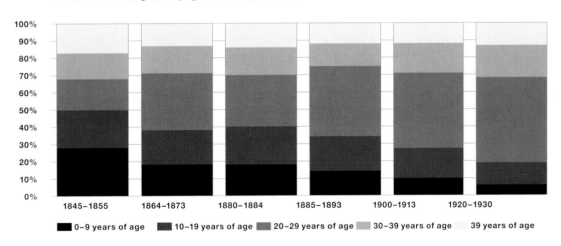

Swiss overseas emigration by profession 1882–1930 (in percent)

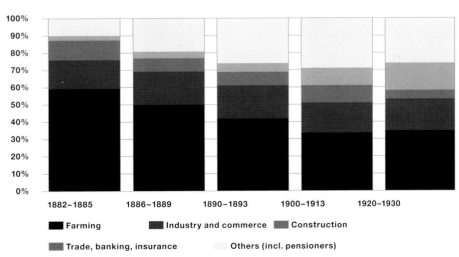

Where they came from

The official statistics contain information about the geographical origins of emigrants within Switzerland. This means cantonal data, as a rule, although in this case information by district is also occasionally available. On the basis of the available figures Switzerland can be divided into 36 regions, and the average number of emigrants from each region during the 40 years in which the movement was at its peak has been compiled. The figure nationally is 2.7 per thousand: in other words, in the 40 years in the period from 1845 to 1923 in which emigration was at its highest, an average of 2.7 per thousand inhabitants left Switzerland to go overseas. This means a rate of 4.5 to 8.0 per thousand for ten Swiss regions, of 2.2 to 3.8 per thousand for 12 regions, and a rate of 0.6 to 2.0 per thousand for 14 regions. Apart from the Bernese lake district, the western half of the canton of Schaffhausen (Klettgau and the Randen massif) and Laufental in the northeastern Jura, the first group of regions consists exclusively of alpine areas and those containing alpine foothills. This includes the cantons of Glarus and Obwalden, the Bernese highlands, the alpine foothills of St. Gallen, northern Graubünden (Prättigau and Plessur) as well as all of Ticino, with the exception of the Valle di Blenio. The second group contains almost all the German-speaking and roughly half the French-speaking Jura districts, parts of the alpine foothill country of central Switzerland, western Graubünden and the cantons of Valais, Basel-Stadt and Zurich. The third group of regions, finally, includes not only the rural German-speaking districts of the Swiss midlands but also the cantons of Vaud, Fribourg, Jura, Nidwalden, both Appenzells, the Valle di Blenio and the Engadine and neighboring valleys.

What can have been the reason for the unevenness of overseas emigration from the various regions? It is interesting to note that the willingness of emigrants to start over again in the New World is correlated less with confessional identity (a bipartite division in Switzerland) than with topographical and linguistic identity (tripartite). It is surely of central importance that farming and husbandry were practiced under the harshest possible conditions in Ticino and the alpine and foothill districts of German-speaking Switzerland, as well as for a considerable period in the Bernese lake district, in the German-speaking Jura, in the Randen massif and Klettgau. Nature set severe limits on agriculture in the high mountain regions, while in the above-mentioned areas the growing number of "dwarf farms" created by inheritance customs were proving a major hindrance to productivity. This was the number one cause of emigration even in heavily industrialized Glarus, where according to statistics emigration from the primarily agricultural Sernf Valley was many times greater than that from the main valley of the Linth, where cotton factories vied for space. Not surprisingly, places like Engi, Matt and Elm in the Sernf Valley came to be known as "Little Ireland." In western Switzerland, meanwhile, in contrast to Ticino and the German-speaking mountain cantons, significantly better agricultural conditions and a Francophone culture at odds with the "Anglo-Saxon" mentality dampened the will to emigrate.

At the same time, overseas emigration was also quite low in those alpine and foothill districts of German-speaking Switzerland that had at their disposal an alternative demographic safety valve. Wherever European and internal emigration had attained elevated levels, the drive to overseas emigration was less pronounced. This was the case, for instance, in the smallest cantons, Nidwalden and Appenzell Inner-Rhodes, as well as in the Valle di Blenio and the Engadine and tributary valleys. The big cities constituted another exception, where a significant increase in emigration was first recorded in the 1880s in the wake of internal immigrants to the cities from other communes, cantons or countries joining the streams of urban emigrants, and thus massively enlarging them. Unfortunately, Swiss emigration statistics cannot provide us with any insight into the motives for such "staggered migration."

More can be determined about the status enjoyed by the United States among emigrants from the various regions. Although inter-regional comparisons are necessarily confined to the period between 1816 and 1913, a close correlation with topographical and linguistic distribution can once again be discerned. The emigration from the cantons of Bern (highlands, lake district, Laufental), Schaffhausen (Klettgau and the Randen massif), St. Gallen (southern alpine foothill districts), Graubünden (Prättigau and Plessur), Glarus and Schwyz, which was heavy and occasionally very heavy, was headed almost exclusively for the United States. Emigrants from western Switzerland, Valais, the big cities and certain rural districts were less unified in their destination, with emigrants from the cantons of Geneva, Vaud and Jura often giving the United States a wide berth, while those from the bilingual and Catholic-conservative cantons of Fribourg and Valais for the most part actively sought alternative destinations. Of the French-speaking cantons, only Neuchâtel sent a medium volume of emigrants to the United States, although it must be noted that many of the people listed as emigrants from that canton had in fact moved there from German-speaking districts of the neighboring canton of Bern.

The native tongue of the inhabitants of Italian-speaking Switzerland had no influence at all on the destinations chosen by its emigrants. Northern Ticinese emigrants tended to favor the United States, while their southern compatriots chose Latin America and Algeria and those from the Poschiavo region emigrated for the most part to Australia. The Valle di Blenio was entirely unaffected by the trend to overseas emigration, rigidly fixated as it remained on emigration to Switzerland's European neighbors as well as to other Swiss cantons.

Research into the history of migration patterns connects long-term orientation to particular destinations with trans-generational "traditions of migration," which in Switzerland have tended to affect mostly German-speaking family emigration to the Midwest as well as central and southern Swiss individual emigration to the Pacific coast of the U.S.

Swiss overseas emigration by region per 1000 inhabitants 1845–1923

(annual mean of major waves of emigration)

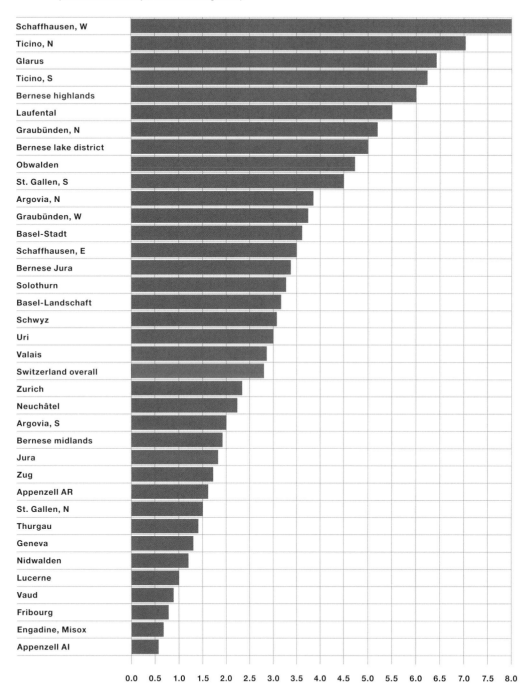

Schaffhausen, W	
Ticino, N	
Glarus	
Ticino, S	
Bernese highlands	
Laufental	
Graubünden, N	
Bernese lake district	
Obwalden	
St. Gallen, S	
Argovia, N	
Graubünden, W	
Basel-Stadt	
Schaffhausen, E	
Bernese Jura	
Solothurn	
Basel-Landschaft	
Schwyz	
Uri	
Valais	
Switzerland overall	
Zurich	
Neuchâtel	
Argovia, S	
Bernese midlands	
Jura	
Zug	
Appenzell AR	
St. Gallen, N	
Thurgau	
Geneva	
Nidwalden	
Lucerne	
Vaud	
Fribourg	
Engadine, Misox	
Appenzell AI	

0.0 0.5 1.0 1.5 2.0 2.5 3.0 3.5 4.0 4.5 5.0 5.5 6.0 6.5 7.0 7.5 8.0

E= East
N= North
S= South
W= West

Emigration to the United States by region 1868–1913

(in percent of total emigration from each region)

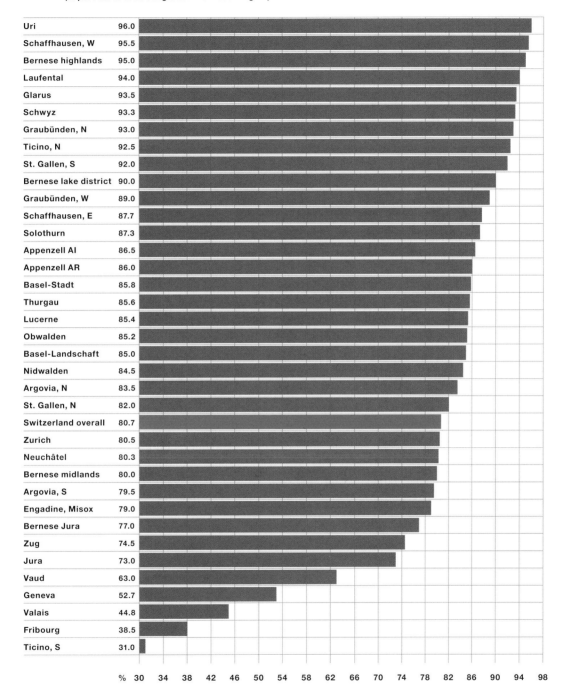

Region	%
Uri	96.0
Schaffhausen, W	95.5
Bernese highlands	95.0
Laufental	94.0
Glarus	93.5
Schwyz	93.3
Graubünden, N	93.0
Ticino, N	92.5
St. Gallen, S	92.0
Bernese lake district	90.0
Graubünden, W	89.0
Schaffhausen, E	87.7
Solothurn	87.3
Appenzell AI	86.5
Appenzell AR	86.0
Basel-Stadt	85.8
Thurgau	85.6
Lucerne	85.4
Obwalden	85.2
Basel-Landschaft	85.0
Nidwalden	84.5
Argovia, N	83.5
St. Gallen, N	82.0
Switzerland overall	80.7
Zurich	80.5
Neuchâtel	80.3
Bernese midlands	80.0
Argovia, S	79.5
Engadine, Misox	79.0
Bernese Jura	77.0
Zug	74.5
Jura	73.0
Vaud	63.0
Geneva	52.7
Valais	44.8
Fribourg	38.5
Ticino, S	31.0

% 30 34 38 42 46 50 54 58 62 66 70 74 78 82 86 90 94 98

E = East

N = North

S = South

W = West

Where they went

The geographic distribution of Swiss immigrants in the U.S. can be derived from American census figures, although the reliability of this census, taken every ten years, is impaired to a certain extent by the fact that it equates national origin with country of birth, and thus does not include as foreign the children born to immigrants after they had arrived in the United States.

These data show that there were 13,000 persons born in Switzerland living in the United States in 1850, 89,000 in 1880, and 125,000 in 1910. These numbers then begin to drop: 113,000 in 1930, 72,000 in 1950, and, in 1970, fewer than 50,000 native Swiss for the first time in more than a century.

Over the course of decades, the celebrated American frontier moved ever further westward before coming to a standstill in the late 1880s in the Great Plains and the Rocky Mountains. A second frontier separated California from the surrounding states before beginning to move to the north and east. The data show that this shift of settlement areas also affected the geographic distribution of Swiss immigrants.

At the same time, the east coast had lost none of its magnetic appeal, likely due to the fact that overseas emigration from the mid-1880s on involved mostly industrial and service workers and no longer comprised small farmers hungry for land. A study of the professional make-up of Swiss colonies overseas commissioned

Regional distribution of Swiss natives in the United States 1850–1930 (in percent of total Swiss natives)

Legend: Ohio, Illinois, Wisconsin, Missouri, Remaining Midwest, Southern States, New York, Remaining East Coast, California, Remaining Far West

in 1938 by the secretariat for Swiss expatriates showed that, apart from those already of retirement age, most of the Swiss then resident on the east coast were employed in the mechanical or service industries.

Around the middle of the 19th century, the Swiss colonies were clustered in the states of New York, Ohio, Illinois and Wisconsin. Almost a quarter of Swiss immigrants lived in Ohio, which offered excellent conditions for the export of meat and grain, followed by 14% in New York, 12% in Illinois and 9% in Wisconsin, where some years earlier immigrants from the canton of Glarus had founded the colonies of New Glarus, New Elm and New Bilten. Louisiana, too, boasted a significant Swiss colony around 1850, although the system of plantations and slave trade upon which the southern states depended had doomed them to economic stagnation long before the outbreak of the Civil War, while the liberal market economy spreading through the east and west of the country was encouraging the growth of prosperity there.

In the 1850s and 1860s, German-speaking Swiss immigrants to North America settled in growing numbers in Missouri, Indiana and Iowa, as well as in New Jersey and Pennsylvania on the east coast. For their part, emigrants from Ticino went their own way. In the 1850s Ticino found itself in an extremely precarious situation, both politically and economically, after General Radetzky of Austria had imposed a total economic embargo on the canton in response to its anti-imperialist sympathies and expelled 6,500 Ticinese from Lombardy. When word got around that another "General," namely the adventurer Johann August Sutter, had found large quantities of gold on his ranch, a veritable mass exodus from the Maggia, Verzasca and Leventina Valleys got underway, bound for California. At around the same time, the siren call of the yellow metal was also emanating from Australia, and a second stream of gold-diggers began to issue forth from the barren mountainous terrain of northern Ticino. Many of the young men who headed for Australia were doomed to die in the mines there, and others returned, exhausted and broken, to their native villages. While the California gold rush turned out to be no picnic either, most of the immigrants there managed to move into more solid employment and thus laid the foundation for a new and entirely sustainable tradition of emigration. Indeed, thousands of northern Ticinese arrived in California in the period from 1851 to 1925; in the 1860s the California fever spread to the foothills of central Switzerland and, in the ensuing decades, to the German-speaking districts of the Gotthard massif as well (Oberhasle, Goms and Hinterrhein). At the same time, other states in the Far West, such as Oregon and Nevada, began to attract young male would-be emigrants, with the result that the stream of Swiss headed for the American Pacific coast grew gradually broader.

The great wave of emigration during the 1880s led to an increase in native Swiss population in almost all regions of the U.S. Most immigrants went to the Far West, which saw its share of native Swiss in the U.S. rise to 17% by 1890, a proportion that increased to more than 22% in 1910 and to as much as 30% in 1930. This phenomenon was, however, due not only to the more intensive direct immigration from central and southern Switzerland but also to bouts of internal migration on the part of Swiss already resident in the United States. In 1930, California and New York were home to almost a third of all Swiss registered in the American census for that year, while Ohio, Illinois and Wisconsin together had only a fifth. The Swiss presence in the United States had thus shifted during the period between 1870 and 1930 from the Midwest to the two coasts, with the Pacific coast the preferred destination for most of those in quest of a new homeland.

Literature and sources

Bundesblatt der Schweizerischen Eidgenossenschaft, **vols. 1851–1920.**

Office of Statistics of the Canton of Bern (ed.), *Statistisches Jahrbuch für den Kanton Bern,* **vols. 1870–1877.**

Office of Statistics of the Canton of Bern (ed.), *Statistische Mitteilungen,* **vols. 1883–1922.**

Rechenschaftsberichte kantonaler Behörden (Bern, Glarus, Solothurn, Schaffhausen, St. Gallen, Graubünden, Aargau, Tessin und Wallis) für die Jahre 1845–1923.

Ritzmann, Heiner (ed.), *Historische Statistik der Schweiz,* **chapter E, Zurich 1996, pp. 364–379.**

Ritzmann, Heiner, *Alternative Neue Welt: Die Ursachen der schweizerischen Überseeauswanderung im 19. und frühen 20. Jahrhundert,* **Zurich 1997.**

Swiss Federal Archives, *Bestände unter E 2 sowie Bestand E 7175 (A) 2 (Fichen der Auswanderungsagenturen für die Jahre 1910–1958).*

Swiss Federal Department of Statistics, *Statistische Lieferungen,* **vol. 1885, appendix II, pp. 103–108.**

Swiss Federal Department of Statistics (ed.), *Statistisches Jahrbuch der Schweiz,* **vols. 1891–1970.**

Swiss Federal Emigration Office, *Die überseeische Auswanderung in den Jahren 1886–1939.*

Illustration

P. 150 Zurich main railway station, c.1930: a couple goes abroad, hoping to build a new future.

Short Biographies

The following biographical sketches, which make no claim to comprehensiveness, give a broader view of Swiss immigration to the U.S. Arranged in chronological order, these brief biographies round out our chronicle of several centuries of emigrants to the United States, driven by a host of forces.

Diebold von Erlach (1541–1565)

Scion of Bernese aristocracy; sent at the age of 17 to France for training at court; returned briefly to his parents; took part in a French expedition to Florida in 1564; made officer; skirmishes with natives; died 1565 in Florida, probably fighting the Spanish. Von Erlach was the first Swiss to set foot on American soil.

Jean-Pierre Purry (1675–1736)

Treasurer of Boudry and mayor of Lignières (in today's canton of Neuchâtel); went to Paris as a speculator; declared bankruptcy; attempted to establish vineyard in South Africa; unsuccessful colonial project in Australia; received land grant in South Carolina and, beginning in 1730, lured more than 300 Swiss settlers there. Most of those who fell for his unscrupulous propaganda and moved to Purrysburg either perished there or moved elsewhere. The settlement no longer exists.

Henri Louis Bouquet (1714–1765)

Son of an innkeeper and merchant, grew up in Vaud, then controlled by the Bernese; entered foreign military service, first for Holland, then for the English crown; sent as lieutenant colonel to the American colonies in 1756; adopted native military tactics and established a form of light infantry; victorious at the battle of Bushy Run in 1763, thus opening the way to the west; skilled negotiator; wanted to return to Switzerland but was promoted to commander of Florida in 1765; died of yellow fever soon after arriving in Pensacola.

Joseph Schantz (1749–1813)

Originally from the canton of Bern, where he was probably known as "Tschanz," emigrated in 1769 to the American colonies; devout Anabaptist; donated a large part of his farmland in 1801 to found the town of Conemaugh, renamed Johnstown ("Schantz-Town") in his honor in 1834. Today, Johnstown in western Pennsylvania is a regional center with a population of 24,000.

Jean-Jacques Dufour (1767–1827)

Son of a vintner from Châtelard (canton of Vaud), emigrated to the U.S. with his brother Daniel; first settled in Kentucky (1796), then in Indiana (1802); introduced European vines in the hope of developing American viticulture; after initial success, the vines fell victim to a blight. The vineyard has vanished, leaving the town of Vevay (named for Vevey on the Lake of Geneva) in Switzerland County, population today a little over 1,500.

Kaspar Köpfli (1774–1854)

Studied in Fribourg; medical practice in Neuenkirch (canton of Lucerne); liberal politician; imprisoned for a few weeks as a suspected French collaborator (1814); moved to Sursee; emigrated to the U.S. for political reasons in 1831 at the age of 57; together with his 13 companions founded New Switzerland in Illinois. The thriving settlement was later renamed Highland and was a popular destination for Swiss emigrants. Today the town has a population of around 9,000.

Henry Detwiller (1795–1887)

From Langenbruck in the canton of Basel-Landschaft; studied medicine, at first with private tutors, then at the University of Freiburg in Germany; emigrated to the U.S. in 1817 and settled in Allentown, Pennsylvania; successful medical practice and pioneering work in natural healing; co-founder of the North American Academy of the Homeopathic Healing Art (1828), now the Hahnemann Medical College of Philadelphia; an enthusiastic natural scientist, assembled a valuable collection of rare botanical and zoological specimens.

Louis Rodolphe Agassiz (1807–1873)

Son of a pastor from Môtier (canton of Fribourg); early education in Switzerland, studies in Germany; physician and natural scientist; worked for several years in Paris; important work in field of ichthyology; professor and researcher in Neuchâtel; published Ice Age theory (1840); after the failure of his printing business emigrated in 1846 to Boston; numerous research expeditions; chair of geology and zoology at Harvard University; founded a natural history museum (1858) and established the National Academy of Sciences (1863); held anti-Darwinian position; countless publications; in short, the perfect scholar.

Lorenzo Delmonico (1813–1881)

From Mairengo in the canton of Ticino; emigrated to New York in 1831; helped out his uncles Giovanni and Pietro Del-Monico (as the name was originally spelled) in their newly opened restaurant; expanded the family business and made of Delmonico's restaurants a meeting place for New York's high society. "The Great Lorenzo" used only the finest ingredients, introduced scores of new dishes and, as Bill Bryson puts it in Made in America, added "the dimension of elegance to American Dining."

Henry Wirz (1823–1865)

Born in Zurich as Hartmann Heinrich Wirz; commercial training; sentenced to four years in prison for embezzlement (1845); pardoned after one year and expelled from Switzerland for 12 years. Went first to Moscow before heading to the U.S. (1849); various jobs in Massachusetts, Kentucky and Louisiana; signed up in the Confederate Army in 1861, became a sergeant, was badly wounded; assigned clerical and administrative duties; beginning in February of 1864 commandant of the prisoner of war camp at Andersonville (Georgia); unimaginable conditions there – 12,000 dead in one year. After the Civil War was tried as a "war criminal" before a military commission, found guilty and publicly executed.

Karl Bürkli (1823–1901)

Born into a middle-class Zurich family; trained as a tanner; became a socialist during his years as a journeyman in Paris; emigrated to Texas with 30 sympathizers (1855) intending to follow the teachings of the French utopian socialist Charles Fourier there. The international colonists failed miserably in their project. Bürkli returned to Switzerland deeply in debt (1858), worked for a food cooperative and became one of the leading figures in the Zurich workers' movement, without ever making a real political breakthrough.

Anselma Felber (1843–1883)

From Kottwil near Sursee in the canton of Lucerne; ordained a nun at the convent of Maria Rickenbach in Niederrickenbach in the canton of Nidwalden; sent to Conception, Missouri, in 1874 with a group of sisters; fruitful work in schools and parishes; established a convent that was to become the mother foundation of the American Benedictine order.

John Heinrich Kruesi (1843–1899)

Grew up in an orphanage in Heiden (canton of Appenzell); apprenticed as a locksmith; worked as a machinist in Zurich; traveled as a journeyman in Belgium and Holland; emigrated to New York (1870); worked for the Singer Sewing Machine Company; met Thomas A. Edison in Newark, New Jersey (1871) and become one of the renowned inventor's closest assistants; translated Edison's revolutionary ideas into workable products; became General Manager and Chief Engineer of the Edison Machine Works in Schenectady, New York.

Henry Clay Frick (1849–1919)

Born in Pennsylvania a member of the fourth generation of descendants of a Swiss immigrant from the canton of Argovia; went to work early for his grandfather; purchased enormous coal deposits; was a millionaire at the age of 30; joined forces with the steel producer Andrew Carnegie; ruthlessly successful industrialist; responsible for violently putting down the Homestead Strike (1892); spent his later years as an art collector in his villa in Manhattan, today the home of the famous Frick Collection.

Oskar Tschirky (1866–1950)

Emigrated with his parents from La Chaux-de-Fonds to the U.S. (1883). Earned money first as a porter, then as a waiter in New York's Hoffman House; applied for the position of maitre-d at the Waldorf; became head of the restaurant and reception (1893) and is said to have created the celebrated Waldorf salad. "Oscar of the Waldorf" arranged opulent parties and was on first-name basis with the rich and famous, but he turned down the job of Director (1913). After 50 years at the Waldorf-Astoria, "Oscar" was ready for a well-deserved rest.

John Rudolph Freuler (1872–1958)

Son of immigrants from the canton of Glarus; real estate broker in Milwaukee; managed a silent film cinema (1905); founded his own production company, held a stake in the Mutual Film studio as well; in 1916 Mutual signed the first major contract with Charles Chaplin ($10,000 a week for one year, plus $150,000 bonus); in 1918 Chaplin went to First National ($1,000,000 for eight films); one year later Freuler's company went bankrupt.

Herbert C. Hoover (1874–1964)

Ancestors from Oberkulm in the canton of Argovia; born in West Branch, Iowa, into a family of Quakers; studied at Stanford University and worked as a civil engineer in imperial China; Secretary of Commerce under Presidents Warren G. Harding and Calvin Coolidge; elected 31st President of the United States (Republican) in 1928; held responsible for the Great Depression and not re-elected after serving one term in office (1929 – 1933).

Rudolph Ganz (1877–1972)

Born in Zurich; at the age of 12 first performed a public cello solo. Conservatory in Lausanne; guest performer with Berlin Philharmonic; emigration to Chicago (1900); teacher of music at the Chicago Musical College; concert tours throughout the world; conductor of the St. Louis Symphony Orchestra (1921–27); President of Chicago Musical College; composer; champion of modern European music in America with many radio and television appearances on the subject of classical music. Hobby: mountaineering.

Ernest Bloch (1880–1957)

Born in Geneva; musical education there, in Brussels and in Germany; teacher of composition at the Geneva Conservatory (1911–15); emigration to the U.S. (1915); Director of the Cleveland Institute of Music (1920–25), then teacher of music at the conservatory in San Francisco; temporary return to Switzerland (1930); beginning in 1938 lived alternately in Ticino and on the American west coast; composer; considered the founder of national Jewish music; main works: *Trois Poèmes Juifs, Israel, Helvetia.*

Albert Hurter (1883–1942)

Studied architecture in Zurich and art in Berlin; emigrated in 1913 or 1914 to the U.S.; drew cartoons in New York before moving to southern California; applied for a job at Disney Studios in 1930. One of the most brilliant graphic artists of his time, Hurter was made an "inspirational sketch artist" at Disney. His sketches laid the groundwork for many Disney films. Hurter's masterpieces include *Pinocchio* and *Snow White and the Seven Dwarfs.*

Eddie Rickenbacker (1890–1973)

Born in Columbus, Ohio, to Swiss immigrants; race car driver and fighter pilot; set new speed record in the nineteen-teens (134 mph); shot down 26 German fighter planes during the First World War; dubbed the "Ace of Aces" and awarded the Congressional Medal of Honor; later founded Eastern Airlines. Rickenbacker is the American pilot hero par excellence; his life story has been filmed, and a military airport near Columbus was named in his honor.

William Wyler (1902–1981)

Born to a Swiss father and a German mother in Mulhouse, in the Alsace in France; educated in Mulhouse, Lausanne and Paris; went to New York at the age of 18; began as a messenger boy at Universal Studios, worked his way up and moved to Hollywood (1922); worked at first as an assistant director, then as a director and producer of numerous Hollywood classics, including the Oscar-winners *Mrs. Miniver* **(1943),** *The Best Years of Our Lives* **(1947) and** *Ben Hur* **(1959); among the most successful directors ever.**

Yul Brynner (1915–1985)

Born Julius Brynner, citizen of Mörikon-Wildegg (canton of Argovia), to Swiss émigré father and Russian mother in Vladivostok; worked as a trapeze artist at a Paris circus (1933–1937), where he suffered 47 broken bones from falling. Attended acting school. Went to the U.S. (1941) and made it big in the Broadway musical *The King and I* **(1951). An Oscar winner, his best-known films are** *The King and I, The Ten Commandments, Anastasia, The Brothers Karamazov* **and** *The Magnificent Seven.*

Robert A. "Bob" Lutz (born 1932)

Born in Zurich on February 12, 1932; emigrated as a child to the U.S.; studied economics at the University of California in Berkeley; served as a fighter pilot in the United States Marine Corps; began to work in the automotive industry in 1963, first for GM, then for BMW, Ford and the former Chrysler Corporation. Today Lutz is Vice Chairman for global product development at General Motors.

Madeleine May Kunin (born 1933)

Born in Zurich; emigrated to the U.S. at the age of seven; grew up in Pittsfield, Massachusetts; studied history, journalism and English literature at various universities; taught at Trinity College in Burlington, Vermont; elected to the House of Representatives (Democrat) in 1971; first female Governor of Vermont (1985–1991); Deputy Secretary of Education under President Bill Clinton; U.S. Ambassador to Switzerland (1996–1999); memoirs: *Living a Political Life.*

Oliver Stumm (born 1961)

Born in Boston to a Swiss professor at Harvard; returned to Switzerland at the age of 12; studied mathematics at the University of Zurich; considered a pioneer of the Zurich techno-music scene; today lives in New York, where he works as a musician, music producer and DJ. His label, *A Touch of Glass,* **launched Scissor Sisters among other pop stars. A popular DJ in Europe as well as in the U.S., he now routinely commutes between the Old and New Worlds – a new chapter in the history of immigration.**

Milena Moser (born 1963)

Born in Zurich; wanted to be a writer while still a child; apprenticed as a bookseller; kept her head above water with a range of jobs while seeking a publisher, a long and frustrating quest; worked for Swiss national radio and various print media; writer in residence at Zurich's *Tages-Anzeiger* **newspaper; emigrated to the U.S. in 1998; lives as a writer with her family in San Francisco. Best-known works:** *Die Putzfraueninsel, Das Schlampenbuch, Blondinenträume, Artischockenherz.*

Urs Hölzle (born 1964)

Studied computer science at the ETH Zurich (1984–88); took Ph.D. at Stanford University (1994); worked as assistant professor of computer science at the University of California in Santa Barbara; has worked for Google since 1999, initially as Vice President of Engineering, now as Senior Vice President Operations and Google Fellow; is known on the job for his red socks and for his dog Yoshka ("Google's top dog"), among other things.

Martin Gerber (born 1974)

Played hockey junior league for Langnau im Emmental; debuted as a goalie in the second league at the age of 17; accompanied SC Langnau (now SCL Tigers) into the national A league (1998); won Swedish championship with Färjestad (2002) before switching to the National Hockey League (NHL). Teams: Anaheim Mighty Ducks and, since 2004, Carolina Hurricanes. After David Aebischer (Colorado Avalanche and Montreal Canadiens), Gerber is the second Swiss goalie to make it big in the NHL.

Martin Lotti (born 1974)

Born in Fribourg to a psychologist mother and architect father; trained in Vevey and Pasadena (Art Center College); degree in industrial design; has worked since 1997 for Nike in Portland, Oregon, initially as a designer, then as Senior Designer and now as Global Creative Director for Women's Footwear; known for decorating the shoes he designs (sometimes the soles) with the Swiss cross.

Text by Marius Leutenegger / Illustrations by Grafilu

Small Number – Big Impact

Insert

Ben Roethlisberger: *Giant genes from the Emmental*

At 24, Ben Roethlisberger is to the U.S. more or less what Zinedine Zidane is to France: the greatest sports hero of them all. Only Roethlisberger doesn't play soccer, he plays American football – as quarterback for the Pittsburgh Steelers. It was mainly thanks to him that his team won the Super Bowl in 2006, what his compatriots like to call the "American Football World Championship." Since then, his name would be on everyone's lips – if the Americans could figure out how to pronounce it. But seeing as not even Roethlisberger himself has any idea how his typically Swiss name is supposed to sound, he has come to be known simply as "Big Ben." Which is pretty fitting, considering he weighs in at 241 pounds and is 6 feet 5 inches tall.

You can't blame Roethlisberger for pronouncing his name wrong. After all, it's been a while since his family left Switzerland: his great-great-grandfather left Lauperswil in the Emmental in 1873. But Big Ben does get points for being interested in his roots. Reasoning that he owes his tremendous success to his genes, he made a special trip to Switzerland in 2006, where he spent an entire day in Lauperswil. Among other things, he took the opportunity while there to get acquainted with Hornussen, the local sport that tends not to cause fractures (as opposed to football). He agrees that his profession is extremely brutal, but there is compensation for the pain: as a quarterback he earns a basic annual salary of 14 million dollars, plus another 20 million for endorsements. *(IV)*

Jewel Kilcher: *Nearly a superstar*

Jewel Kilcher has sold 30 million albums – around twice as many as top Swiss recording star DJ Bobo, which makes her the most successful musician with Swiss citizenship. But you won't be seeing any inside looks at the star's private life in the *Schweizer Illustrierte,* Switzerland's version of *People* magazine, any time soon. For while the 32-year-old singer appreciates Swiss cuisine and can even sing a Swiss folksong or two, she is a 100% U.S. celebrity. She has had a Hollywood career for some time now, was linked to Sean Penn and is currently going out with Ty Murray, the rodeo star. And the general public knows virtually nothing about her Swiss roots. *Time* magazine called Jewel American pop's new goddess, and in the world's largest celebrity database, IMDB, her father is said to be German. The truth is that Jewel's grandfather on her father's side emigrated to Alaska in 1940 from the Swiss canton of Basel-Landschaft, and her grandmother followed a year later. Jewel's father is a musician, and she started performing publicly with him when she was still a girl. She went on to attend the renowned Interlochen Arts Academy in Michigan and began writing her own songs. Her catchy tunes and slightly sentimental lyrics (with the occasional touch of critique, witness the line "it's not all dirty, but it's not all clean" from her song "Stand") have had mass appeal just to the left of mainstream ever since. Jewel is not a superstar, but she's close: she made *Stuff Magazine's* list of the "102 Sexiest Women In The World" in 1992 – at 92ⁿᵈ place. *(V)*

Bello Nock: *Courageous cartoon character*

While the circus world may be pretty international, it's not especially open. Circus people tend to stick together, and to themselves, and that's why the scions of two of Switzerland's circus dynasties, the Bauers and the Nocks, went to the United States together over 40 years ago, drawn by the promise of bigger Big Tops and higher earnings, as well as, of course, real success in a country in which stars need not be embarrassed to be rich and famous. The two Swiss circus performers remained in the U.S., where Eugen Nock's son, Bello Nock, was born in Florida. Bello was a typical circus kid, making his first public appearance when he was knee-high to a grasshopper and receiving an eclectic education. And while he is now being called America's best clown, that's not all there is to him. He's also a true professional, a world champion on the trampoline, for instance. Bello is always on the lookout for a new challenge. He has hung from a trapeze suspended from a helicopter above the Statue of Liberty, and balanced on a tightrope over Patterson Falls – and of course he still had a smile on his lips and a joke on the tip of his tongue. The redhead's spectacular courage is (nearly) matched by his hairdo, which gives him the appearance of a cartoon character who has just stuck his finger in a socket. The trademark look has helped Bello Nock become a star of Ringling Bros. and Barnum & Bailey, purveyors of "The Greatest Show on Earth," America's leading circus spectacle. Sadly, he is hardly ever to be seen in Europe, although he did make it to the Old World once, in 1998, when he was awarded a prize at the celebrated Monte-Carlo Circus Festival. (*VI*)

Renée Zellweger: *The Swiss girl from Norway*

Renée Zellweger is truly a citizen of the world. Her mother, from whom she gets her cheekbones and eyes, is a member of the Sami, a Norwegian minority numbering some 70,000. Her last name, meanwhile, comes from her father, Emil Erich Zellweger, who emigrated from Au in the Swiss canton of St. Gallen to Australia after the Second World War. Renée's parents met on a ship bound for the U.S., and the product of their union is Hollywood's most successful ugly duckling. Renée has made a career out of portraying figures beyond the conventional conception of glamor. In *Bridget Jones,* for example, she delighted millions of women by struggling to lose the 25 extra pounds she had carefully gained for the role. And in *Chicago* she played a no-talent daydreamer who wants to become a star. Renée crammed ten months long for the part, going from being a non-dancer and non-singer to garnering an Oscar nominee for her performance. One year later, in 2003, she won the Academy Award for best supporting actress for her appearance in *Cold Mountain.* Unfortunately, in accepting this distinction she did not include herself on the short list of Swiss Oscar winners, saying in an interview instead that she was proud to be Norwegian. Darn. Switzerland could be proud of this woman, who knows what she wants. For example, in 2005 she married country singer Kenny Chesney, only to announce their separation just four months later. Her reason? Fraud! She wanted children, Chesney didn't. The marriage did not end in divorce, but was instead annulled, meaning that Ms. Zellweger is still single… (*VII*)

Steve Ballmer: *Microsoft cheerleader*

If Bill Gates is the face of Microsoft, then Steve Ballmer is the brains behind it. The two men met at Harvard. Gates dropped out after a year to found Microsoft, while Ballmer stayed and completed his studies. Gates brought Ballmer to Microsoft in 1980. The PC revolution, which virtually no one had predicted, earned Microsoft untold wealth in the form of licensing fees. Microsoft owes its meteoric rise in large measure to Ballmer, who turned out to be a canny businessman and visionary and helped make his company one of the most valuable in the world – as well as making of himself the American Dream in person, the fulfillment of every immigrant parent's wishes. His father, Fritz Ballmer, grew up in Basel. After the war he worked as a translator at the Nuremberg Trials, where he came into regular contact with Americans and decided to emigrate to the U.S. Steve was born in Detroit in 1956. Although he is able to speak a few words of German and occasionally spends his vacations in his father's homeland, Steve Ballmer is the very picture of an American entrepreneur – both an aggressive competitor and a sensitive manager, he is what *Forbes* has called "Microsoft's cheerleader and chief executive." Success means everything to him. His bonus program for Microsoft employees has made millionaires out of many of them. Ballmer himself, of course, is a billionaire, one of the 25 wealthiest people in the world. (*VIII*)

Further Reading

Anderegg, Klaus et al., "Zu Stand und Aufgaben schweizerischer historischer Wanderungsforschung," *Schweizerische Zeitschrift für Geschichte,* vol. 1987, pp. 303–332.

Arlettaz, Gérald, "Emigration et colonisation suisses en Amérique 1815–1918," *Studien und Quellen (Zeitschrift des Schweizerischen Bundesarchivs),* vol. 1, 1975, pp. 31–95.

Basler, Konrad, *The Dorlikon Emigrants. Swiss Settlers and Cultural Founders in the United States,* Swiss American Historical Society Publications, vol. 10, New York, 1996.

Blocher, Andreas, *Die Eigenart der Zürcher Auswanderer nach Amerika (1734–1744),* diss. University of Zurich 1976.

Brunnschweiler, Dieter, *New Glarus, Wisconsin: Gründung, Entwicklung und heutiger Zustand einer Schweizerkolonie im amerikanischen Mittelwesten,* Zurich 1954.

Cheda, Giorgio, "Aspetti dell'emigrazione ticinese in California," *Studien und Quellen (Zeitschrift des Schweizerischen Bundesarchivs),* vol. 28, 2002, pp. 277–298.

Cheda, Giorgio, *L'Emigrazione ticinese in California,* vol. 2, Locarno 1981.

Hauser, Walter, *Bitterkeit und Tränen: Szenen der Auswanderung aus dem Tal der Linth und die Ausschaffung des heimatlosen Samuel Fässler nach Amerika,* Zurich 2002.

King "Küng," Joseph, *Als Schweizer noch das Weite suchten: Autobiographie eines Schweizer Emigranten (1860–1934),* Glarus 1993.

Lätt, Arnold (ed.), *Schweizer im Ausland: Von ihrem Leben und Wirken in aller Welt,* Geneva 1931.

Lobsiger, Georges, "L'émigration de Suisse pour outre-mer de 1887 à 1938," *Le Globe, Organe de la Société de Géographie de Genève,* vol. 1946, pp. 31–61.

Lüönd, Karl, *Schweizer in Amerika: Karrieren und Misserfolge in der Neuen Welt,* Olten 1979.

Mesmer, Beatrix (ed.), *Der Weg in die Fremde / Le chemin d'expatriation,* Itinera, vol. 1992.

Métraux, Guy, *Social and Cultural Aspects of Swiss Immigration into the United States in the Nineteenth Century,* New Haven, Connecticut 1949.

Perret, Maurice Edmont, *Les colonies tessinoises en Californie,* diss. University of Lausanne 1950.

Pfister, Hans Ulrich, *Die Auswanderung aus dem Knonauer Amt (1648–1750). Ihr Ausmass, ihre Strukturen und ihre Bedingungen,* diss. Universtity of Zurich 1987.

Ritzmann, Heiner, "Der Homo migrans und die Macht der Tradition: Die schweizerische Überseemigration im 19. und 20. Jahrhundert– Knacknuss für Wanderungstheoretiker," in Andreas Ernst et al. (eds.), *Kontinuität und Krise: Sozialer Wandel als Lernprozess,* Zurich 1994, pp. 61–81.

Ritzmann, Heiner, *Alternative Neue Welt. Die Ursachen der schweizerischen Überseeauswanderung im 19. und frühen 20. Jahrhundert,* Zurich 1997.

Schelbert, Leo, "Die Wanderungen der Schweizer: Ein historischer Überblick," *Saeculum* 28 (1967) 4, pp. 403–430.

Schelbert, Leo (ed.), *New Glarus 1845–1970: The Making of a Swiss American Town,* Glarus 1970.

Schelbert, Leo, "Einführung in die schweizerische Auswanderungsgeschichte der Neuzeit," *Schweizerische Zeitschrift für Geschichte,* supplement no. 16, Zurich 1976.

Schelbert, Leo and Hedwig Rappolt (eds.), *Alles ist ganz anders hier: Auswanderungsschicksale aus zwei Jahrhunderten,* second edition, Olten 1979.

Schelbert, Leo, *Swiss Migration to America: The Swiss Mennonites,* New York 1980.

Schelbert, Leo, "Swiss Americans," in Judy Galens et al. (eds.), *Gale Encyclopedia of Multicultural America,* vol. 2, New York 1995.

Schelbert, Leo (ed.), *America Experienced: 18th and 19th Century Accounts of Swiss Immigrants to the United States,* Camden, Maine 1996.

Schweizer, Max, *Bilder aus Neu-Schweizerland (1831–1900): Werden und Wachstum einer schweizerischen Einwanderersiedlung in den Vereinigten Staaten von Nordamerika (Madison County, Illinois),* Zug 1978.

Schweizer, Max, *Neu-Schweizerland: Planung, Gründung und Entwicklung einer schweizerischen Einwanderersiedlung in den Vereinigten Staaten von Nordamerika (Madison County, Illinois),* diss. University of Zurich 1980.

Spyri, Johann Ludwig, *Gutachten über die schweizerische Auswanderung an die Schweizerische Gemeinnützige Gesellschaft,* **Zurich 1865.**

Steinach, Adelrich (ed.), *Swiss Colonists in 19th Century America,* reprint, with new introduction and indexes by Urs-Peter Schelbert, Camden, Maine 1995.

Steinemann, Ernst, "Die schaffhausische Auswanderung und ihre Ursachen; ein Beitrag zur Wirtschaftsgeschichte," *Zeitschrift für Schweizergeschichte,* vol. 1934, pp. 310–359 / 401–450.

Sutton, David H., *One's Own Hearth is Like Gold: A History of Helvetia, West Virginia,* **Swiss American Historical Society Publications, vol. 8, New York 1990.**

"Swiss," in Stephen Thernstrom et al. (eds.), *Harvard Encyclopedia of American Ethnic Groups,* **Cambridge and London 1980.**

Swiss-American Historical Society (ed.), *Prominent Americans of Swiss Origin,* **New York 1932.**

Tritt, Donald G., *Swiss Festivals in North America: A Resource Guide,* **Morgantown, Pennsylvania 1999.**

Vogel, Hermann, *L'émigration suisse hors d'Europe dans l'entre-deux-guerres (1919 à 1939),* **Lausanne 1947.**

Von Grueningen, John Paul (ed.), *The Swiss in the United States: A Compilation prepared for the Swiss-American Historical Society,* **Madison, Wisconsin 1940.**

Wessendorf, Berthold, *Die überseeische Auswanderung aus dem Kanton Aargau im 19. Jahrhundert,* **Basel 1973.**

Addresses / Links

Association for a Swiss Migration Museum:
www.migrationsmuseum.ch

Organisation of the Swiss Abroad:
www.aso.ch

Swissemigration – Information and consulting service for Swiss nationals abroad and emigrants provided by the Swiss Federal Office for Migration:
www.swissemigration.ch

Swiss Federal Department of Foreign Affairs:
www.eda.admin.ch (see particularly "Auslandschweizerdienst")

Swiss Federal Office for Migration:
www.bfm.admin.ch

Swiss National Museums:
www.musee-suisse.ch

Swiss Roots:
www.swissroots.org

Your Gateway to Switzerland:
www.swissworld.org

Contributors

Editors

Bruno Abegg
Born 1965; doctorate in geography from the University of Zurich; researcher and freelance journalist, with special interest in tourism, climate change and migration; lived and worked in Wisconsin from 2003 to 2005, where he studied Swiss immigration.

Barbara Lüthi
Born 1969; studied history at the Universities of Fribourg, Basel and Tel Aviv; research fellow at the University of Basel; special interest in migration and U.S. history.

Markus Hodel
Born 1954; lawyer; many years as legal advisor to the city of Winterthur (integration issues); founding President of the Association for a Swiss Migration Museum (MIG). Cultural event planner, Managing Director of MIG and head of the Ellis Island project.

Authors

Bernard R. Bachmann
Born 1939; descendant of Swiss immigrants to the U.S.; secondary-school diploma (classics); since retiring as a computer technician and product manager, has devoted himself to his passion for writing and has published an acclaimed book about Johann August Sutter.

Thomas Buomberger
Born 1952; doctorate in history; author and journalist for a variety of Swiss print periodicals; member of the board, Association for a Swiss Migration Museum; author of *Kampf gegen unerwünschte Fremde. Von James Schwarzenbach bis Christoph Blocher* (The war against unwanted foreigners: From James Schwarzenbach to Christoph Blocher), Zurich 2004.

Bänz Friedli
Born 1965; stay-at-home husband and freelance writer; since 1983 work for press, radio and TV; special interest in pop culture and sports; author of major pieces on the influence of migration on the development of folk and pop music.

Erika Hebeisen
Born 1966; studied history at the University of Zurich; doctorate in history and research fellow at the University of Basel; special interest in the history of memory, youth movements, modern gender history and the 1968 generation.

Annelise Leuenberger
Born 1972; schoolteacher; studied history at the University of Bern; masters in history, with frequent work on the topic of migration; currently research fellow at the Murten Museum and specialist in adult education.

Marius Leutenegger
Born 1966; journalist, copywriter, family man and theater-lover with a penchant for historical and social material as well as for portraits and travelogs.

Stephan Lütolf
Born 1975; studied history at the Universities of Zurich and Lausanne; masters in history; works as a writer/producer for Swiss national radio DRS 3; various research projects for the "Small Number – Big Impact" exhibition.

Guido Magnaguagno
Born 1946; served as Deputy Director of the Zurich Kunsthaus; currently Director of the Tinguely Museum in Basel; has mounted exhibitions of work by Robert Frank, with whom he has been friends for many years.

Roland Müller
Born 1944; doctorate in business psychology; research and teaching at the ETH and the University of Zurich; work as a business and communications consultant and editor in chief of management magazines; one of his ancestors founded a factory in Warren (Rhode Island) in 1870.

Walter Niederberger
Born 1954; studied German literature, business and media studies at the University of Bern; since 2002 economics and UN correspondent for the *Tages-Anzeiger* in New York.

Barbara Rettenmund
Born 1965; studied history at the University of Basel; masters in history; work on various exhibitions, theater and book projects.

Heiner Ritzmann
Born 1958; studied history at the University of Zurich; doctorate in history; extensive research work on Swiss migration; since 1999 has worked for the Swiss Federal Statistical Office, Social Security Section.

Jacques Sandoz

Born 1942; photographer and film-maker; worked in the 1970s in Los Angeles; made several feature films; conceived and produced the study *Les Sandoz: une famille des montagnes neuchâteloises à la conquête du monde* (The Sandoz family: today the mountains of Neuchâtel, tomorrow the world), 2000.

Leo Schelbert

Born 1929; emigrated to the U.S. in 1959; doctorate from Columbia University in New York; taught American history at the University of Illinois in Chicago (1971–2003); professor emeritus; noted expert on the history of Swiss emigration.

Jürg Schneider

Born 1961; studied history and political science in Basel, Bern and Buea/Cameroon; masters in history; various exhibition and book projects on the subject of historical photography; special interest in west and central Africa.

Urs Widmer

Born 1927; degree in civil engineering from the Swiss Federal Institute of Technology in Zurich; worked for one year in O.H. Ammann's office in New York; engineering firm in Winterthur (1957–1966); Mayor of Winterthur (1966–1990); since retiring has written studies of local history as well as of the history of engineering.

Illustrator

Grafilu

Founded in 2004 by Pascal Staub, Grafilu stands for drawing with passion and two-dimensional creations.

Photographer

Mathias Braschler

Born 1969, studied geography and modern history before turning to photography. Lives and works in New York and Zurich.

Picture editing

Tiberio Cardu

Born 1952 in Italy, emigrated to Switzerland, where he experienced the fundamental change in relations between native Swiss and foreign residents. Photography Editor at *Das Magazin* (1991–2005) and other periodicals; agent, curator and exhibition planner.

Graphic Design

Anne Hoffmann

Born 1944 as a Dane, since 1969 in Switzerland; graphic designer (HfG Basel); has run own design studio since 1986. Areas of artistic and cultural activity: book and catalog design, corporate design, poster design. (Assistants Iris Baumann, Linda Baumann)

Picture Credits

André Saunier Louis Chevrolet Watch Company 78, 79, 81, 82, 83
BBB Mss.Mül 466 (3a), Mss.Mül 466 (1) 37, 38
Cinémathèque Suisse 101, 140, 141
ETH-Bibliothek Image Archive Zurich / Estate of Othmar Ammann 84, 87, 88
Fritz-Zwicky-Stiftung Glarus 106, 109
General Motors 80
Grafilu Insert 168 IV-VIII
Ken Ross 127, 128
Keystone 16, 20, 21, 23, 25, 26, 89, 93, 95, 96, 143, 150
Keystone / Ann Ronan Picture Library 50
Keystone / INDEX 55
Keystone / Marty Heisey 33
Keystone / Niklaus Stauss 123
Keystone / SPL 56
Keystone / Sylvain Grandadam 31
Keystone / Walter Bieri 122
Kunstmuseum Solothurn 51
Museum of New Mexico, courtesy Palace of the Governors (MNM/DCA) 72, 75
Mathias Braschler 1, 2, 3, 4, 15, 28, 173, 174, 175, 176
National Library 43
Privat collections 97, 104
Port Authority of New York 84
Reto Camenisch 132, 135, 136, 137
Sacramento Archives & Museum Coll. Center / NZZ Libro 49
Swiss Alpine Museum 146
Swisspress 44
Swisspress / Caroline Sandoz Pifer Collection 89, 102, 103
Swisspress / Solomon R. Guggenheim Museum Archives New York 61, 62, 63
Swisspress / Landov 45
Swisspress / William Kilcher Collection /Pratt Museum Homer, Alaska 112, 114, 115, 117
Wisconsin Historical Society 66, 68, 69